MAKING
LOVE
MEANINGFULLY

MAKING
LOVE
MEANINGFULLY

The Purpose of Marital Intimacy

CHARLES AND VIRGINIA SELL

BROADMAN
&HOLMAN
PUBLISHERS

NASHVILLE, TENNESSEE

0-8054-2719-8

Published by Broadman & Holman Publishers,
Nashville, Tennessee

Dewey Decimal Classification: 306.73
Subject Heading: SEXUAL BEHAVIOR \ MARRIAGE

Unless otherwise stated all Scripture citation is from the NIV, the
Holy Bible, New International Version, © 1973, 1978, 1984 by
International Bible Society. Other passages are noted as NASB, The New
American Standard Bible, © The Lockman Foundation, 1960, 1962,
1963, 1968, 1971, 1972, 1973, 1975, 1977, 1995, used by permission;
and KJV, King James Version.

1 2 3 4 5 6 7 8 9 10 07 06 05 04 03

TABLE OF CONTENTS

ACKNOWLEDGMENT

*A*ll authors are indebted to many people who make the publication of their books possible. We, too, owe a great deal to those who assisted us along the way in getting Making Love Meaningfully into print.

Credit, first of all, goes to Broadman & Holman editor, Leonard Goss, for believing, along with us, that our book was unique enough to be published and would make a difference in the lives of many couples. We are also grateful to Kim Overcash for the work she did as project editor to make this book the best it can be.

Our gratitude goes out to all the staff at Broadman & Holman for the fine, professional job that was done and that will continue to be done on this title to glorify the Kingdom.

We owe the most to the many couples who through our survey, counseling sessions, and marriage seminars shared with us private matters of their sexual relationships. Thanks for helping us understand better the problems and needs of couples in their marriages. May this book help many couples "make love meaningfully."

—Charles and Virginia Sell

PREFACE

$\mathcal{T}$alking about intimate issues such as sex is difficult for many couples. Yet, improving your lovemaking requires frank communication. Reading a book can help facilitate your discussions and enable you to reach some agreement in your thinking about your physical relationship.

Making Love Meaningfully is somewhat unique. While most books about marital sex explain what we do, this one focuses on why we do it. We will help you go from the purpose of sex to your practice of sex, which we believe is a Christian approach.

My husband, Charles (nickname: "Chick"), based this book on more than four decades of teaching and writing about marriage and family. During that same period we've conducted scores of marriage seminars in which we've learned a lot about the intimate issues couples face by fielding hundreds of questions about sex. And in counseling sessions, many couples have given us a glimpse of this private part of their lives.

In addition, Christian students in the graduate school where Charles teaches told us about their marriages through a survey that we conducted. After describing attitudes toward sex that were brought into marriage, they explained how they dealt with negative ones. Most of them reported having had thoughts and feelings that interfered with their sexual adjustment. The majority of them (80 percent) reported that they combated these hindrances by gaining a biblical perspective. And most of these learned, by reading, to think Christianly of their physical relationship.

Basically, what helped many of these couples was realizing that marital sex should be *purpose-directed*. They believed that lovemaking is a gift of God that he designed for certain reasons. *Making Love Meaningfully* describes these purposes and then describes explicitly how aiming for these can make your love life, as well as your marriage, more satisfying, passionate, and meaningful.

We've collaborated in the writing. While Charles has done the bulk of the work, I've assisted in the research, acted as a sounding board, and tried throughout to contribute a woman's point of view. To stimulate your conversation, we've included some creative discussion guides, called "Pillow Talks," at the end of each chapter. We wish for you God's best in your marriage—and in your bedroom.

—Virginia R. Sell

Chapter One

MAKING SENSE
OF THE SENSUAL

WARM SEX, NOT COOL

*A*fter a decade of marriage, if they were asked to describe their sex life, Jerry and Rosalind would say it was "warm." During their marriage's early years, they would have used adjectives such as "hot" or "intense." Not that they don't think about these words anymore. The glossy magazine covers at the supermarket make them all too obvious. Titles of articles promise them sex that's torrid and wild. They wonder to themselves if nice and warm is enough.

Other couples are just as puzzled—some for different reasons. Julia and Mark would label their sex life "cool," not as in "great" but as in "gone." They, like lots of other couples, are going through a period of "sexual cooling," when the stress of work, parenting, and the like have nearly put out their sensual fire. They aren't sure how to heat it up again or even if they should try.

Frederick and Pearl's dilemma is much the same, except that their lovemaking hasn't cooled because it was never hot to begin with. Though in love, they've always had problems making love. Pearl is not turned on in the bedroom. If sexual desire were measured in calories, hers would rank with Diet Coke. She and Frederick have just about given up on aiming for lukewarm sex, let alone hot.

1

None of these couples actually exist as named. Yet, as a marriage counselor and seminar leader, I've talked to enough people about their marriages to know there are many like them who wonder if there's enough excitement in their bedroom. In the midst of a sex-crazed culture where media of all sorts constantly remind them of the kicks and thrills of passion, most couples will eventually think: "Our sex life could be better." It could happen at any time in the course of a marriage: a few years after the wedding, after settling down in a job, after having a child, reaching midlife, going through menopause, or the onset of the empty nest.

They may then decide to turn up the heat in their bedroom. Some succeed, but others don't, their efforts often making the situation worse because they don't always agree on how to do it. If one of them refers to magazine articles and books that promise fantastic sex via positions and erotic oddities, the disagreement might intensify. Disappointment and hurt mixes with confusion, causing them to go in any number of directions. They might separate or stay together, settling into a mediocre union, turning outside the home for something meaningful to fill the void of an empty marriage. They settle for what they have, putting energy into raising children and other activities instead of into creating a more passionate relationship.

When couples respond negatively to their loss of sensual fervor, they miss a great opportunity to improve it, along with their marriage. Claims prominent sex therapist Jack Morin: "More often than you might think . . . diminishing sexual desire is a sign of growth . . . in such cases lost desire is not a problem to be fixed but a message to be heeded."[1]

Dissatisfaction signals a turning point in marriage. It is a time for making things better, not settling for less. Because of today's increased life span, your marital journey will probably last more than fifty years. To sustain it for so long a time, you will need to make the trip exciting, which includes, in part, continually fueling the flame of your sensual relationship.

Sex doesn't have to be boring. If we can believe the surveys, there are just as many married twosomes who still find excitement between the sheets—many of them members of AARP—as those who don't. The secret, if there is one, is strategy.

Many have taken the wrong approach to fix their bedroom blahs. Too much attention is given to the erotic techniques of sex and not enough to what really matters. Never before has so much information been available about making love. We know a lot about how to position ourselves, where to touch, when to touch, and how to touch (women enjoy circular strokes, men straight ones, for example). It was the so-called sexual revolution that set us plummeting in this direction. During its most ferocious years, the publication of *The Sensuous Woman* typified the attitude toward sex. In this best-seller, the author, Joan Garrity, described her sexual exploits, vividly explaining to women how to have sex with anyone, anywhere, anytime, and any way. The stress was on the ravishing of bodies, not the relating of persons. Erica Jong's famed novel, *Fear of Flying*, had the same message. In it the central character's fantasies include having a quick romp with a stranger, suggesting that sex is best when it is quick and anonymous, devoid of emotional attachments.[2]

It seems that this baby boomer viewpoint continues. Today's young adults, the so-called X-generation, agree. A new study released by Rutgers University's National Marriage Project found young Americans prefer casual sex and low-commitment relationships, believing sex is for fun with no strings attached.[3] They passionately pursue bodily sensations, attempting to squeeze every ounce of sheer sensuality devoid of any personal relationship. "Hooking up" is their expression for having sex. Sex on campus is often about as personal as "two airplanes refueling."[4]

THE GREAT OMISSION

What this approach omits is the most significant feature of sexual relating: what it means to those who are doing it. Casual sex stresses the linking of bodies; holistic sex stresses the connecting of persons. Satisfying—even fantastic—sex is sex that is meaningful. Doing it for the right reason is what makes it sizzle.

Eventually, even Joan Garrity apparently came to realize this. In an interview, years after penning *The Sensuous Woman,* she said, "I have now found that the best sex is with someone you love." After promoting sex without love, she has concluded that sleeping at home is much better than sleeping around.

Many men and women want to discover what Joan Garrity has. They are yearning to link sex with love, some after experimenting too long with separating them. Instead of merely making out, they want to make love. If the experienced Joan Garrity is right, this is how to have the "best sex." This is because the significance of sex, like other human acts, is embedded in its meaning.

Like many couples, my wife and I often read in bed before turning out the lights to sleep. During that time, one of us often reaches over and massages the other's neck and shoulders. The relaxing of taut muscles and stirring of nerves that radiate warm currents throughout my body make this a welcome treat for me. But my enjoyment of Ginger's pampering is due to more than the physical pleasure it gives. I also relish the warm messages I know her hand and fingers are conveying to me: "I love you," "I care for you," "I understand you."

In some cases, the meaning of bodily contact between individuals far surpasses any physical sensation it creates: a hand on the shoulder, for example. Hardly felt, it can tell someone without words, that you want to comfort, encourage, or show your appreciation to him. While Ginger and I know everyone recognizes that these contacts are gestures that convey some message, we have found that couples don't consider carefully the meaning of their sexual contacts. Yet that is what makes them so special. Ask yourself: "Do you want a kiss or do you want what a kiss means?"

Having sex without meaning is like watching your baseball team play in September with no chance to make the play-offs. There may still be plenty of action, but when it doesn't mean anything, it takes the edge off the excitement. When the team's still in the running, when every game counts, the air is electric, each pitch dramatic, each hit exciting.

This is not to say that meaningful sex is always electrifying or that casual, impersonal sex is always dull and tedious (just as no Chicago Cubs' game is to its fans); otherwise, it wouldn't be so tempting. When Diane Keaton said to Woody Allen, "Sex without love is an empty experience," he replied, "Yes, but as empty experiences go, it's one of the best."[5]

In a good marriage the physical and the personal relationship are connected. Counselors and sex therapists call this the "second language of sex," and as never before, they are trying to teach people how to speak it. Isolating sex from its personal meaning creates one of two problems—each destructive but in opposite ways.

Love's Facsimile

Overemphasizing the erotic is the first destructive process. Relegating sex to physical titillation alone leads to frenzied attempts to satisfy sensual hunger by erotic thrills. This effort to maintain the erotic edge drives the quest for more raw eroticism. Books and articles advise couples to explore the outer limits of lust, not love. To do this they may view steamy videos, try a sex toy, leaf through triple-X magazines, act out a secret fantasy, make love in a different location, or test a scorching new position.[6] The only way to increase the satisfaction is to accelerate the intensity, either through novel approaches or new partners. But soon one runs out of options or finds that exploring the outer limits may be extremely dangerous. It also leads to boredom. "I am burned out with sex" is a common statement from men and women in their early thirties who have learned that their senses alone cannot offer unlimited pleasure.

As the insightful Rollo May put it, "[Sex without love] conveys only a facsimile of love, as many a person has found the morning after."[7] Married couples who follow this formula expect sex to carry the weight of a marital relationship, which it is unable to do. No wonder a partner can feel betrayed. One woman told us, "The only time my husband says he loves me is during sexual intercourse." Thinking that being in bed with his wife is the same as being in love with her, this husband failed to recognize that sex is an expression of love, not love itself.

We're not suggesting that couples should shun good erotic technique. But marital sex cannot thrive on technique when it is devoid of love, intimacy, and other feelings. These feelings provide the richness and intensity of lovemaking. This is not to say that good sex is not part of a good marriage. In fact, a healthy marriage makes great sex possible. Blending lust and love makes for good sex and a great marriage. That combination offers not only satisfaction but also infinite variety and fulfilling freshness. No matter how creative a person is, methods to express lust are limited; ways to love are not.

Taking the Sex Out of Love

Disconnecting love from sex is only one way to isolate it; another is to degrade sex as mere eroticism. Sex is relegated to something subhuman (animal-like) or nonhuman (demonic). This negative attitude is usually bred in an antisexual atmosphere in one's childhood family. Sex therapists are well acquainted with people whose parents passed down their disgust with sex as a family heirloom. Other people think badly of sex because their sex education lacked a wholesome view. Because parents, pastors, or teachers said little about sex, the sources of these people's sexual knowledge were dirty jokes and pornographic magazines and movies. This approach made sex into something suspicious, secretive, and seamy.

Christians have sometimes contributed to this tainted view. Many of them have been influenced by a viewpoint that started in the early church. In the third century, Augustine, a theologian honored by Catholics and Protestants, denounced sexual passion, thus poisoning the stream of Christian thought for centuries. To read what he wrote about sex is like scanning a manual on cattle breeding. "Nothing so casts down the manly mind from its height as the fondling of a woman in those bodily contacts," he wrote.[8] He claimed that the only justification for having sex is to have babies; intercourse without the intent to conceive a child is a kind of sin. In all his discussion Augustine never integrates sex with love, companionship, or intimacy, let alone enjoyment.

To claim that God created sex only for conceiving children strips sex of its other purposes and reduces it to a physical act, turning love-making into mere copulating. This is a vicious form of compartmentalization, and it has tragic results. It can lead to spurning one's own sensuality and to an intense frustration for the partner who is the victim of this rejection. For example, if a woman returns from a satisfying honeymoon, she will likely say, "My husband is so wonderful," rather than, "Sex is so wonderful." Surely sex was exhilarating. But sex was not an impersonal, physical act; it signified a personal union with her husband. If, however, sex was not enjoyable, the wife says, "I don't like sex." She may not realize that she has compartmentalized sex. She is saying that she really doesn't enjoy her husband, since she dislikes his sexuality. Unless she fathoms this, she may not understand the deep hurt her rejection creates in her husband. Our attitudes toward sex are projected onto our spouse because sex is a whole-person matter. If a woman thinks sex is dirty, she thinks her husband is, and he is going to feel the brunt of that attitude.

UNCOVERING THE REASONS GOD CREATED SEX

To understand the connection between our humanity and our sensuality we must determine what sex means to our marital relationship. Social scientists who wonder why sex for humans is different from that of animals are attempting to make those connections. They've found that humans have sex for recreation, but animals do so for procreation (only dolphins and a few other animals have recreational sex). Also, most animals are generally promiscuous, while humans have loving, monogamous relationships.

Evolutionary scientists have posed an answer that is popularized by today's media. At one time humans were much like animals; their babies were fully developed when they were born and able to care for themselves. Eventually this changed, and babies, as they do today, came into the world in an immature stage. They needed many months of care to reach a stage of maturity comparable to that of other animals at birth.

The sacrificial care that mothers provided evolved into human love. But, because mothers could not rear children alone, they needed someone to provide food, shelter, protection, and social support. Reliable extended family could do this, but eventually fathers took up the task. The father was coaxed into assuming this responsibility by emotionally bonding with the mother, the pleasure of face-to-face sex playing a major role in this emotional bonding.

Eventually this physical pleasure led to the emergence of emotional love, which, it has been discovered, has a biochemical basis. Women experienced it first. Breast-feeding and cuddling their babies released in women a neurochemical called oxytocin, producing in them a feeling of warm affection. Men too get jolts of oxytocin, not from children but from women. During sexual climax, oxytocin increases from three to five times its normal level in men. Thus the ultimate reason for love between the sexes is to foster parental investment of time, energy, material resources, and love in the human infants.[9] This theory is speculative, and it may contribute something to understanding ourselves. (At least it puts new meaning into the idea of chemistry between lovers.) But it falls far short of explaining the complexities of human love.

Imposing meaning on things is difficult for science, confined as it is to a secular viewpoint. For meaning, we must turn to something beyond secular theory. As William Kilpatrick has wisely insisted, "The secular has a need for the sacred. The sacred view of life is not simply an alternative within society; it is indispensable to society. To step away from it is to step into the void."[10] Life without some spiritual viewpoint is senseless, and as Christians, we can turn to Scripture to make sense of life—and of sex.

The way we make sense of the sensual is to uncover the reasons God created it. From the Scriptures I will describe six purposes for human sexuality and devote a chapter to each. These purposes, transcending sex and offering us some reason for what we are that comes from outside and beyond ourselves, are

1. Intimacy: "It is not good for the man to be alone" (Gen. 2:18).
2. Procreation: "Be fruitful and increase in number" (Gen. 1:28).
3. Love: "I will give you my love" (Song of Songs 7:12).
4. Affirming our identity: "God created man in his own image, . . . male and female he created them" (Gen. 1:27).
5. Pleasure: "God . . . richly provides us with everything for our enjoyment" (1 Tim. 6:17).
6. Deterring immorality: "Since there is so much immorality, . . . the husband should fulfill his marital duty to his wife, and likewise the wife to her husband" (1 Cor. 7:2–3).

Taken together, these purposes portray a high view of sex and a practical one as well. Woven into the fabric of a couple's relationship, these purposes produce an exquisite marital tapestry. This is no doubt why studies repeatedly confirm that religious people claim to have greater sexual satisfaction in marriage. Editors of *Redbook*, which reported this finding, surmised that religious women enjoy sex more than other women do because they accept it as a part of God's creation. Thinking about sex in God's terms is a major step toward thinking holistically about it.

Now let's turn our attention to making love meaningfully. There are four steps to the process that you should be prepared to take as you read.

Realize That Sex Begins in the Mind

First you should be prepared to change your thinking, where necessary. Making love is more mental than it is physical. Or, as some people crudely put it, "Sex begins in the head, not the bed." Although the names are altered, the following comments represent attitudes that we often hear in counseling sessions.

"Though Rosalind and I are very much in love and extremely close friends, our sex life isn't all that great," Jerry confides. "The kind of pas- sion I would like to have just isn't there. Something's wrong, and I can't figure out what."

"Is it OK for me to fantasize about being raped when Mark and I are making love?" wonders Julia. "It's the only way I can climax. Some friends advised me to do this, and it works. But I'm not sure it's the right thing to do."

"Pearl is disgusted with sex and has been for all our married life, says it's animal-like." I remember Frederick's downcast expression as he explained the cause of the bitter argument he had just had with his wife. She rarely accepted his sexual advances, and he was frustrated and angry.

Each of these scenarios shows how the most important sex organ is the brain, or the heart, if you prefer. Most of us harbor attitudes that need discarding.

The closeness without passion that Jerry describes is the most difficult to explain, since it is commonly thought that sex and intimacy go together. For this couple, however, the two are separated. No doubt this attitude began in childhood, when one of them was excessively intimate with a parent. Perhaps Rosalind's mother died or left, and Rosalind took her place in her father's emotional, though not sexual, life. Etched in Rosalind's brain is the idea that closeness with a man not only excludes physical inti- macy but also forbids it. In marriage she feels more like a sister than a lover to her husband. Sex for them takes on an ambience of incest.

Julia, the young wife who needs to imagine being assaulted, also thinks about sex in a different way. Her brain tells her sex with anyone is forbidden. To deal with her guilt, she gives herself permission to turn on only when someone takes sex from her. Julia needs a major mental makeover.

So does Pearl, who relegates sex to the animal kingdom. Yes, mam- mals and humans have sexual similarities, but to degrade human love- making because of this is twisted thinking (besides being an insult to animals). Anything humans do is human, even when it's immoral. Of all the violations persons are accused of in Scripture, none is described as acting like an animal. How you think about sex makes it right or wrong. To paraphrase Yogi Berra's humorous quip, half of having great sex is 90 percent attitude.

Despite the recent surge of research on the physiology of sex, sex therapists still believe sex is more a matter of heart than of body. Our bodies sometimes need fixing, but our minds need it more. Perhaps our parents, uncomfortable with their own sensuality, or afraid of a child's, made their children feel ashamed for having sexual thoughts or feelings. Not treating the child's natural curiosity about her sexuality as wholesome and helping her enjoy the wonder of it, the parents made her feel uneasy or guilty. For some people the negativity is more serious, deeply implanted by sexual or emotional abuse. Whatever its source, this self-incrimination keeps many couples from the exhilaration of spontaneous, unhindered physical expressions of love. As sex therapist Jack Morin put it, "Guilt is second only to anxiety as the world's foremost antiaphrodisiac."[11]

However wrong or severe our ideas may be, most of us harbor some unhealthy attitudes toward sex.

It is a mistake to think these feelings are given by God to guide us. Our consciences can point us in the right direction, but they are not always reliable. Our consciences can be distorted, making us feel bad about doing something good and good about doing something bad. The apostle Paul recognized this when he warned us about the teachings of false prophets: "They forbid people to marry and order them to abstain from certain foods, which God created to be received with thanksgiving" (1 Tim. 4:3). They do this, says Paul, because their "consciences have been seared as with a hot iron" (1 Tim. 4:2). The searing doesn't mean that something has been burned out of their consciences. Rather, something has been burned in because the hot iron is a branding iron. In the deep inner self, these people have been stamped with the wrong concept: marriage is bad. Like computers that have been wrongly programmed, our consciences need to be reprogrammed.

Sometimes this is difficult to do because the negative impression is so severe. A woman once told me she could not have intercourse with her husband without severe pain. Doctors told her that the problem was in her mind, not her body. As she related stories from her childhood, I could see why. When she was only four years old, her grandfather had been the first to violate her, exposing himself to her in the cab of his truck and ordering her to play sexual games. In her early teens another relative had repeatedly forced himself on her. Embarrassed and afraid to tell her parents, she stored her disgust in her mind. Now, though she wants to make love with her husband, her body won't let her, tightening her vagina to keep him out. As a Christian, she is aware of Christ's forgiveness and acceptance. But the cleansing of her mind will take time and effort.

Overcoming the past's hold on any of us is usually not easy. Negative thoughts must be confronted again and again. It is as difficult for the conscience to give up its attitudes, formed through the years bit by bit, as it is for the body is to give up excess weight that was added bite by bite. To change our consciences we need the same kind of patience we need to stay on a weight-loss diet. But it is possible to change your conscience, and the place to start is in your mind, as the apostle Paul wrote, "Be transformed by the renewing of your mind" (Rom. 12:2). The blueprint for remodeling the conscience is Scripture. As you ponder the biblical truths in this book, changes will begin to happen.

Discover the Meaning

In addition, you should be prepared to think about what sex means to you. Holistic sex, as we have seen, is much more than a collection of urges and acts. Our erotic self is intricately connected with our hopes, expectations, feelings, struggles, desires, and anxieties—everything that makes us human. Whereas sexual intercourse is simple, passionate lovemaking is complex. A luxurious sensual relationship will result from the interplay of your erotic acts *and* your personal relationships.

Therefore we should evaluate what we are getting out of our sexual relationship beyond physical pleasure. We should be asking ourselves whether sex makes us feel close, loved, cared for. It is these God-given purposes that will make sex fulfilling. Intense erotic feeling is included—the kind that sometimes goes with so-called quickies. However, there are times when the intensity level is lower but the lovemaking may be better. During a warm, lingering, connecting session, the souls as well as the bodies connect. Of the quickie, spouses might say, "That was really terrific," and of the other, "I really felt close to you tonight."

To evaluate your sex life properly, you need to appreciate the difference between these two types of lovemaking. Feeling extremely close may be far more satisfying to you than feeling intensely passionate. Exploring the meaning of what you do in your bedroom might help you understand and accept better your preferences as well as those of your partner. After some thought, you may discover that you favor a certain position not because it's more sensually exciting but because it's more personally intimate.

Insights such as this can help you and your spouse better handle conflicts over what you each prefer. Men and women commonly differ, for example, on how they connect intimacy with sex. Men seek intimacy through sex, while women desire intimacy with sex. A woman wants to do things that make her feel close before she jumps into bed, which a man is in a hurry to do. Preliminaries to him are like singing the national anthem before the first pitch: a patriotic duty that delays the start of the game. What women may not understand is that sexual intercourse makes most men feel close to their wives. Desmond Morris, a prominent anthropologist, surmises that men want sex because they want to be hugged, something they don't experience much in other contexts.

Thus a husband may want to make love more frequently than his wife does, something she attributes more to his lust for pleasure than his need for intimacy. "All he wants is food, sex, and TV, not necessarily in that order," one wife complained. However, if she realizes that his appetite for sexual intercourse is a hunger for intimacy, she may be better able to interpret his advances.

What is true of this one example of holistic thinking will be true in countless other ways. You will learn to discover and appreciate the richness of your total sexual experience. Viewed this way, warm sex might not seem mediocre because it carries with it love and intimacy. It may be far superior to the media-hyped "hot sex." This is not to say that trying to turn up the heat in the bedroom is wrong. Rather, I'm suggesting that the way to do that is to focus on its meaning.

Seek the Meaning

Cultivate your sex and marital life by seeking what is meaningful to you. The major purpose of this book is to help you to cultivate your physical relationship by doing those things that fulfill the purposes God intended for sex.

We hope to help men better grasp the connection between sex and personal intimacy, someting hard for some men to understand. In a counseling session, James complained that his wife was not responsive sexually. Maria explained that it was difficult for her to get turned on because he didn't do anything to get her in the mood. He wanted to make love when she didn't feel loved. He was constantly critical of her. An angry man, James would sometimes lose his temper and throw and smash things. When he wanted sex, he would ask for it as if he were requesting Maria to fix him a sandwich. He made no attempt to warm up to her first. James badly needed the introductory course Women 101, which I attempted to teach him. First he needed to see how his anger was hindering his sex life, and then he had to master his anger. He also needed to start affirming instead of abusing his wife. Then he would have to find some ways to make her feel intimate before being passionate: a private dinner together, conversation, some light touching and kissing.

Each chapter of this book will include practical suggestions that grow out of each of the six God given-purposes for marital sex. The possibilities are as exciting as your willingness to be adventurous and as novel as your ability to be creative. But relating sexually will not be without problems. Thinking holistically will help you deal with them, which is the next step in the process.

Deal with the Problems

It will be difficult to solve any sexual problems you may have without thinking holistically about them. Almost always these are problems of the personality or of the relationship. Sex is tied to our capacity to love, to be intimate, to give, to receive, to lose ourselves in another. For this reason researchers John Cuber and Peggy Harroff found that among the couples they interviewed, those who saw sex holistically were "remarkably free of the well-known disabilities."[12]

No matter how small and if it's not physical, a sexual problem can be handled in two ways. First, confront whatever prevents you from having sex for the right reasons and then deal with problems that arise from conferring on sex a wrong meaning.

We will help you with the first set of problems related to fulfilling the purposes of sex. Difficulties with loving or with being intimate can follow a person into the bedroom, just as a poor self-image will. Some people may be able to have sex without intimacy more easily than they are able to have intimacy without sex. For them intimacy is so difficult that they avoid it. This is especially true in the beginning of a relationship, when every exposure is like taking off a piece of protective armor.

There are more insidious reasons for being allergic to closeness. Being rejected during childhood is a major one. When children try to get close to a parent who spurns them, it hurts. That emotional pain causes these children to build up defenses against intimacy just as turtles grow shells. As adults they will avoid being hurt by refusing to get close. This fear of intimacy will show itself in the bedroom. Intimacy is one of the two most legitimate and powerful ingredients of making love. Those who are uncomfortable with it will not be able to relate sexually to their partners with abandon.

People who have been rejected are not the only ones who have some aversion to intimacy. Nor is this the only personality quirk that hinders our sex lives. *Making Love Meaningfully* will touch on many of these and show all of us how to make love for the right reason, no matter how severe our struggle to do so.

Also, this book promises to help with the second type of problem: desiring sex for the wrong reasons. There is a dark side to sex, and sexual deviation, for example, is energized by it. Without love, the rapist uses sex to dominate; the sadistic person, without sensitivity, finds pleasure in hurting. Sex for such persons is a way of acting out their distorted emotional and mental selves.

Some deviations may not have to be that destructive to be a problem. Any sort of wrong association will do: dominating, being dominated, proving one's virility, expressing anger, being naughty, rebelling. Feeling that sex is wrong can turn a person on to sex just as well as it might turn him or her off. That in part is what the proverb may be saying: "Stolen waters are sweet, and bread eaten in secret is pleasant" (Prov. 9:17 KJV).

Morin claims that sexual arousal is related to unresolved issues from the past. A man, for example, who uses sex to abuse and dominate a woman may be acting out of anger bred by an abusive mother. Reading this book will enable you to identify your turn-ons, good and bad. Then you can look into your childhood for clues about why certain things arouse or do not arouse you. Understanding and dealing with any unsettled past issues may be what you need to make sex more satisfying and meaningful.

GET READY

Before we explore God's purposes for sex and the crucial implications for our married life, let's look once more at the steps that lead to holistic sex.

1. *Change your thinking.* What you do in bed depends on what you think. Transform your mind and revolutionize your marriage and the marriage act.

2. *Discover what sex means to you.* Infuse more meaning into your marital sex life. Whatever you are doing, recognize its purpose and get more out of it.

3. *Cultivate your sex and marital life by seeking what is meaningful to you.* Novelty alone will not make for lasting and satisfying sex; novelty with meaning will.

4. *Solve the personal and relational issues behind any sex problems.* Problems in the bedroom are rarely sex problems; they are hang-ups of the personality or the marriage. Improve these and you'll repair your love life.

Sex is OK. This isn't a novel idea cast on the American shore by the waves of the sexual revolution. For centuries biblical scholars have taught this. "Conjugal love is first among earthly blessings that God in mercy gives us. Enjoy then with thankfulness what's yours," wrote Charles Bridges more than one hundred years ago.[13] Sex for the right reason, at the right time, and in the right place is one of God's greatest blessings. You no doubt have the right person and can choose right times and places. Now let's think more about the right reasons.

✥ *Pillow Talk* ✥

This is the first of seven Pillow Talks, one following each chapter. Each is designed to help you talk about the theme of the chapter. Since these sections often deal with sensitive areas of your relationship, skip those Pillow Talks or portions of them that you don't think you are able to discuss yet.

Sex is a language. In fact, sex is the most powerful nonverbal talk. Other forms of verbal and nonverbal speech are superficial by comparison. Through sexual intimacy we send positive or negative messages.

This Pillow Talk will help you better understand these messages. Then you will know better how to continue transmitting the positive ones and even find new ways to do so. You will also be better able to deal with any negative messages. Decoding the language of sex isn't easy. You won't complete it in one session. Expect it to be an ongoing process that you will never fully finish. Besides, the messages keep changing as your relationship unfolds.

On a sheet of paper, write the letters of the alphabet and then a number that signifies the power and frequency of the messages in your sexual life. (By sexual life, we are including acts of touching, casual verbal and nonverbal expressions of the sensual during the course of the day, foreplay, the sexual embrace and variations, and the afterglow time.) You may skip the negative list and concentrate only on the positive if you like. With your lists in hand, begin at the top and share your answers, discussing anything it brings to mind.

Positive Messages of Our Sex Life

VERY STRONG				WEAK	
6	5	4	3	2	1

A. "I want you."

B. "I need you."

C. "I comfort you."

D. "I support you."

E. "I enjoy revealing myself to you."

F. "I enjoy your revealing yourself to me."

G. "I feel a part of you."

H. "I feel as if you belong to me."

I. "I feel as if I belong to you."

J. "I enjoy all of you."

K. "I feel a sense of being totally in union with you."

L. "I feel a spiritual union with you."

M. "I have fun with you."

N. "I forgive you."
O. "I understand you."
P. "I accept you."
Q. "I am patient with you."
R. "I am tender with you."
S. "I care about you."

Negative Messages

T. "I neglect your needs."
U. "I don't understand you."
V. "I dislike part of you."
W. "I hurt you."
X. "I don't respect your feelings."
Y. "I don't respect you."
Z. "I use you."

Chapter Two

SEX AND INTIMACY
LOOKING AT MARRIAGE CLOSE-UP

*M*arna had an insatiable appetite for sex. Compulsively, this unmarried woman seduced every man she could, even salesmen who came to her door. Shame and guilt bred by these impulsive trysts drove her to a Christian counselor. Many sessions later, counseling to that point ineffective, the counselor decided that her obsession for raw sex was actually a deep yearning for intimacy. He suggested a solution: "Find three friends who will give you a hug every day." Blushing, she replied, "I would be too embarrassed to ask anyone to do that." Before the counselor could fully fathom a woman who could ask a stranger for sex but not a friend for a hug, she continued. "But I could give three hugs a day." She did, and she got three intimate hugs back. Her compulsion vanished.

That a treatment so simple should work so well shouldn't surprise us. Sex and intimacy are bound together as vitamin C is to orange juice. Sex is meaningful in large measure because intimacy is. Our lust for physical contact, a mark of our culture, is perhaps most of all a deep yearning for personal closeness.

NOT AN OPTION

God has built this desire into us. He made us so that we can't be human alone. After creating Adam, God said, "It is not good for the man to be alone" (Gen. 2:18).

What studies we have of adult loneliness also tend to confirm this. Besides emotional stability, physical health and even immunity to disease may be linked to the quality of one's relationships. Psychologist James J. Lynch has discovered a relationship between weakened family ties and physical illness. He found that the amount of serious illness was significantly less among people who had deep relationships with other family members than among those whose relationships in the family were superficial. "Simply put," he concludes, "there is a biological basis for our need to form human relationships."[1]

MARRIAGE IS CLOSE WORK

One of those relationships occurs in marriage. In response to Adam's aloneness, God announced, "I will make a helper suitable for him" (Gen. 2:18). The solution to man's unhealthy solitude was Eve—not an animal, not another male, not even God himself. This doesn't mean that marriage is the only place to find companionship. Other relationships can satisfy our need for intimacy. In general, this passage tells us that Adam by nature was a social creature who needed human contact. Yet, specifically, the passage does designate the male-female union as a significant and special form of intimacy. The famous theologian John Calvin, three centuries ago, saw this: "The combination of husband and wife in body and soul is intended to help man overcome his aloneness," he wrote.[2]

Not everyone agrees with this explanation. "Adam was not drooping about, overcome with loneliness, yearning for a companion," claims Mary Pride. "How could he be lonely, face to face with God?" she continues. "God did say, 'It is not good for the man to be alone,' but the reason He gave was that Adam needed a helper. God could have given Adam a dog if all Adam needed was a companion. God could have given Adam another man if companionship was all Adam needed." What Adam needed, she concludes, was a female to be the mother of his children in order to fulfill God's command to populate the earth. "Intimate marriage isn't biblical," she asserts. "Intimate marriage demands that marriage be self-centered. It insists that kicks and thrills are the reasons for marriage. It tries to squash everyone into one mold—that of hedonistic teenagers—and destroys all who can't fit."[3]

I can understand this writer's concern, but I can't agree with her conclusion. She worries that people who seem to have little capacity for intimacy and romance will be hurt if these ideals are made a norm for marriage. But we shouldn't abandon ideals because they might be hard to achieve. Clearly God intended for sex and marriage to be intimate. The very words used to describe marriage are redolent with the idea of intimacy: "For this reason a man will leave his father and mother and be united to his wife, and they will become one flesh" (Gen. 2:24). The phrase "be united" (*dabaq* in Hebrew) depicts precisely what the word *intimacy* means to us today: a passionate, close relationship that involves a person's soul and body.[4] Even the phrase "one flesh" portrays an intimate, personal union. In Hebrew the term "flesh" *(basar)* does not refer to merely the body, as it does in English. Rather, it sometimes includes the whole person. Thus in this passage "one flesh" means a union that is both physical and personal.

Even the Old Testament word for sexual intercourse, *yada,* implies that sex is never just a physical act. Unlike a vulgar English word for the same act, *yada* literally means "to know." Rather than using *yada* only as a euphemism to avoid embarrassment, the Hebrews normally used a word to mean intellectual knowing because they believed sexual intercourse involves a deep intimate knowledge of another.

Other Scriptures also stress this intimate side of marriage. In Proverbs 2:17, "the term for the closest possible human relationship is used for the husband. *Aloof,* rendered **partner** in some translations, means *intimate friend.* In dramatic fashion, the passionate woman in the Song of Songs confirms this same idea in her poetic pronouncement: 'This is my lover, this my friend, Oh daughters of Jerusalem' (5:16)."[5]

True marital intimacy requires exposing our souls. Just as we peel off our clothes layer by layer to reveal our bodies, so we should disclose bit by bit our thoughts and feelings. Animals mate; humans meet.

Bodies linked, exploring each other passionately in the
private spheres of our once-secret sensuality.

Eyes locked, searching each other intensely in the personal
regions of our ever-mysterious souls.

The gush of erotic feeling between our senses.

The flow of our spirits into one another.

The wild, ecstatic screams or deep-throated whimpers.
Not mere clamor of uncontrolled lust but songs of delight composed and performed only for me.

Isn't this the feeling of closeness that makes us return to our lovemaking again and again? Isn't it then that we sense so profoundly that we are not alone?

MAKING THE CONNECTION

From this understanding of the link between sex and intimacy flow all sorts of suggestions for our loving and our lovemaking. The first one touches a crucial, often problematic, area of marriage: communication.

Watch Your Language

Having heard enough of the television newscast, Jack slipped into bed beside Marsha, who was relaxed but still awake. A subtle movement of his hand on her breast told Marsha that Jack was interested. A scant small turn of her shoulder indicated she was not. At this Jack grunted and brusquely rolled over, leaving a two-foot gap between them. It was now obvious to both that his gonads were shouting "charge" but her hormones were signaling "retreat." To herself Marsha said, "What's the big deal? He's angry." Jack too was talking to himself: "What's wrong with her? She doesn't understand my feelings and needs. This really hurts."

This couple needs to realize that they are carrying on a dialogue without words. Sex talks because through it we come to know each other. Sex is a language that cannot be matched by words or perhaps another act. Only a gesture of violence, punching someone in the nose, for example, can send as forceful a nonverbal message.

Marsha needs to realize that her rejecting Jack's sexual advances is a big deal. Certainly she should feel free to do so, and Jack should grant her that freedom. But both she and her husband need to recognize that the subtle shifts of their bodies away from each other pack powerful messages.

Though these nonverbal messages can often be loud, they are not always clear. They are often puzzling and misunderstood. Marsha interprets Jack's advance as a desire for pleasure. He deciphers her brush-off as insensitivity to his needs. To her, his rolling over and grunting means anger. Maybe he isn't angry, just disappointed, and that she should be able to accept. The problem is that she doesn't understand what he is feeling, and he doesn't understand her feelings. They need to talk with words to correct the garbled messages they are sending with their actions.

They also need to learn how to send the right sensual messages. By warmly rolling over to Jack's embrace, kissing, touching, and eventually joining with him, Marsha is carrying on a warm, positive dialogue that can convey all sorts of messages. "I love you; I like being with you; I enjoy responding to you; I like your responding to me; I like revealing myself to you; I delight in your revealing yourself to me; I care for you; I respect you." But a neglected or inhibited sex life can send negative messages. A man who has a low sex drive may tend to forget about his wife's needs and may unknowingly be saying he doesn't care about her. A woman who can't disrobe in front of her husband is saying, "I don't want to reveal myself to you." In various ways scores of hurtful things can be said: "I don't like you; I reject you; I think you are oversexed; I don't enjoy being with you."

The point is this: If your sex life is good, you send good messages; if it's bad, your messages are negative too. Cultivating what you do to each other sensually improves what you say to each other personally. A couple with serious sexual difficulties may need time to solve them and thus send the right nonverbal messages. But until they achieve sexual harmony, they will need to communicate a lot of positive messages in other ways to overcome the negative messages they are sending in bed.

Improve Your Aim

Another practical guideline grows out of the link between sex and intimacy: Couples should seek all types of intimacy in their relationship, not just the sexual. The reason for this is that intimacy is the greater need. And even though raw physical sex is a form of intimacy, it is not complete. We can be joined physically while remaining emotionally unattached, leaving us feeling detached and alone. However, whenever we bring to our beds a feeling of closeness, our physical lovemaking can soar to greater heights of intensity.

There's an irony in this. If our goal is to have a better sex life, we must not make sex our major goal. Rather, superior sex results from giving priority to intimacy instead. Yet married people, most often men, make sex the goal of their relationship, and most aspects of the relationship fit into that. If we were to put how they think into the form of a chart, it would look like this.

CHART A

GOAL IS SEXUAL INTERCOURSE

Activities increase in intimacy, heading toward sex

Placing arm around her waist   Deep kissing

Going for a walk together   Heavy petting

Looking into each other's eyes

 Goal: Sexual Intercourse

Talking about their relationship

Talking about making love

Reasoning from this chart, a man, for example, thinks like a football quarterback. Wanting to score, to get his wife in bed, he plans: "I'll start with a walk around the lake. That will get me to the thirty-yard line. Then I'll put my arm around her waist," and so on. If he's smart, like a well-prepared quarterback, he will have read the scouting reports on women to know what plays to call and what moves to make. To the chart-A thinker, intimate acts are foreplay, things you do or tolerate to get to what matters: sexual intercourse, or, for those who take this viewpoint to the ultimate extreme, orgasm.

Chart B, on the next page, displays a better way to think about how other intimate acts relate to sexual ones.

CHART B

GOAL IS INTIMACY

Activities have varying degrees of intimacy
and can be ends in themselves

Walking together   Looking into each other's eyes

Cuddling   Kissing

Hugging

—————————————⟶   Goal:
Intimacy

Talking about the relationship

Talking about life's meaning

Praying together

Sexual intercourse

Making intimacy a major goal will give couples some crucial advantages over those who follow chart A. They will improve their feelings of closeness by permitting each other intimacies that are not always connected to sex. Recognizing that a walk around the lake or a candid talk by the fireside need not always lead to the bedroom frees couples to enjoy these things for themselves. Otherwise they may not indulge in these unless sex is possible or wanted. A wife, for example, may yearn to cuddle next to her husband while watching television. However, if she knows this will make him want to charge into the bedroom, she may choose not to do it if for some reason she doesn't want to go all the way. Both partners are cheated because snuggling by itself has its rewards.

These contacts will help satisfy the intense longing for closeness. Wives especially will benefit from this, according to conventional wisdom. It's usually thought that women take part in sex to get intimacy, while men accept intimacy in order to get sex. Pierre Mornell, a prominent psychiatrist, popularized this idea in *Passive Men, Wild Women*. Couples who come for counseling have the same plot to the stories they tell. The husband comes home at the end of the day, plops down in front of the television, and does little to connect with his wife. But wives want something more from their husbands, and they tell them so. For husbands, however, demands for longer talks and honest expressions of feelings add up to one thing: pressure. More of that they don't need, so they withdraw and retreat and lapse into sullen silence. They get more passive as their wives get more hysterical.[6]

While this author is correct, it also seems to be true that many men enjoy and desire intimacy. In our marriage seminars, when we ask men and women to list what they want more in their sexual relationships, men, as often as women, report that they would like their partners to be more intimate in ways other than physical ones.

Both husband and wife can learn to appreciate small but potent intimacies: a warm glance, a hand on the shoulder, a knowing smile, and lingering smells, tastes, and memories of each other. A friend of mine tells me that playing tennis with his wife is an intimate experience. "Across the net, without saying a word, we exchange all kinds of thoughts and feelings through the faces we make and the casual glances we give. If someone were watching us," he says, "they would have no idea that all of that was going on between us."

Take the Broad Road

Once our focus is on intimacy, we can view it as a city with scores of highways leading to it. Sometimes it includes sharing the bad as well as the good things of life.

INTIMACY IS
Sharing the pleasures of the bedroom or
Enduring with another the pain of a hospital room.
A long talk about life or
A knowing glance across the room.
Sharing the joy over a newborn baby or
Grieving together over a stillborn one.
Sitting silently in the sunlight or
Walking in the rain.
Praying for non-Christian friends and relatives or
Sacrificially giving to support world missions.
Cuddling or
Arguing.

Getting a back rub or
Being kidded.
The novelty of a new bride or
The familiarity of a bald head.
Spirited conversation or
Comfortable silence.
The fragrance of a favorite perfume or
The pungent odor of someone else's medicine.

Talk with your mate about the kinds of activities that make you feel close, and plan to do more of them. You have a wide range of choices. There is sensual intimacy, which may not always include genital union: holding hands, sitting close, kissing, hugging. A timely touch on the arm or a hand on the shoulder may create a powerful feeling of nearness.

Perhaps the most profound intimacy comes when we allow someone else a peek into the caverns of our soul. Call that *communication* intimacy, composed of the telling of secrets, sharing of personal emotions, and disclosure of hopes, visions, and plans.

Intellectual intimacy offers great rewards: discussing a book you both read, sharing your concept of God, arguing about politics, discussing new ideas.

Another route to take is *emotional* intimacy: making each other laugh, standing by while one of you cries, being happy or depressed together. Something like an illness can make a couple feel close as he listens to her complaints and nurses her with care.

Then there is *social* intimacy: enjoying the company of the same people, meeting with a small group, enjoying a party, or playing together with the children.

Recreation begets intimacy: winning a game or losing one, bird watching, or hiking. Some couples draw near to each other by jointly creating something or working and serving together: planting a garden, redecorating the house, refinishing a chair, team teaching a Sunday school class, helping with a local fund drive or political campaign.

Intimacy also has a *spiritual* dimension: worshiping at church together, praying as a couple, studying God's Word, talking of your faith and doubts.

People differ on what makes them feel close. For some couples, praying together or talking offers more intimacy than sex. Not all couples will experience all types of intimacy, nor will they want to. One couple, because of different religious beliefs, may have little spiritual intimacy. Another couple may not care to work or serve together. Teaching a Sunday school class or wallpapering the dining room together may create more conflict than closeness. What's important is that you try to acquire intimacy in ways that are most satisfying to you.

Create an Accepting Ambience

When we ask couples what keeps them from being close, they almost always list first the fear of rejection. All of us have strange feelings and thoughts we aren't proud of. If we tell about our sexual fantasies or weird feelings, we're afraid someone will think badly of us. But as a husband and wife become more comfortable with each other, they will be able to share more and more of these private thoughts, bizarre or silly as they might be. When this happens, each will feel more loved and accepted, appreciated for what they are, not for what they were supposed to be. Ginger and I have shared personal thoughts with each other that we once thought we never would—only after many years of slow, painstaking opening up to each other. People are like groundhogs: when they stick their heads out of their holes and sense the slightest bit of hostility, they quickly pop back inside. We can't expect our spouse to be vulnerable if we are going to criticize or laugh whenever she is. A judgmental look can be enough to silence our partner. Even worse is using against a partner some secret she's shared. "I once told my husband I felt insecure," a woman told me. "Ever since then, he tries to win arguments by throwing it back at me: 'The problem is you're just insecure.' I wish I'd never told him."

I eventually learned that I had to stop being critical of Ginger if I was going to get her to talk with me. In the early years of our marriage, I made it difficult for her to share her ideas and opinions. When she did, I usually questioned them or offered what I thought were better ones. For example, when she would give her explanation of a Scripture verse, I would often say something like, "But that's not what the Greek says." She soon had enough of that, deciding to avoid any dialogue that would permit me to hurt her. Periodically I would complain that I would like to have more conversations about serious matters with her. It took many years for me to agree that I was the cause of her restraint. Since then I've tried to stifle my criticism and show more respect for what she has to say.

Accepting also includes projecting that we do care about what our partner is revealing to us. People have told me they have clammed up to their spouse because they've been ignored. I have often heard remarks like, "I don't share my feelings because my husband doesn't care how I feel."

To Thine Own Self Be Kind

Opening up to each other will require learning to accept ourselves as well as our mate. Sometimes our reluctance to bare our soul is due more to the attitude we have toward ourselves than the attitude of our partner toward us. Shame shuts us up, sometimes when it is uncalled for. Normal human feelings embarrass us. We feel badly that we get angry, depressed, jealous, suspicious, or disappointed, and we hesitate to admit to these emotions. But there is nothing inherently wrong with these feelings. In certain situations it's OK to be angry or jealous. God himself sometimes feels this way. Yet false ideas about what it means to be human keeps us from admitting how we feel.

When she speaks to women, Ginger often relates how, in the early years of our marriage, she was afraid to tell me about her periodic times of depression. She's a happy person, but a small bout with the blues was part of her monthly menstrual cycle. As a young wife, she hid her down times from me, thinking that being cheerful was part of her job description. Keeping it from me, however, made her feel lonely and even more depressed. Two years into our marriage, she summoned the courage to tell me how dejected she felt. Not knowing what to expect, she said, "Chick, I am really feeling down." I didn't condemn her or quote a Bible verse about her needing to rejoice in the Lord. I simply said, "Here's a shoulder to cry on," and opened my arms to her. Of that moment Ginger says, "As those arms folded around me, we were both aware that our relationship had jumped to a new level of intimacy."

To be open to each other requires our accepting the whole range of human emotions. If you are embarrassed to stand naked before a mirror, you will not feel good about being exposed to your spouse. What is true of nakedness in the physical realm is also true in the personal. If you're not able to accept your inner self, with its contradictions and follies, you will have a hard time sharing your self with others. To be intimate, we need to come to grips with who we are and learn to forgive and accept what we find. Then we won't have to hide behind masks of dishonesty and silence.

Self-disclosure is risky business for anyone. "Intimacy is always difficult," claims one expert. "If it isn't difficult, it isn't intimacy." Getting closer to each other will involve taking the chance that your partner might not respond favorably. Risks, however, don't have to be big ones. Try sharing or doing things just a bit above your comfort zone. If your partner doesn't respond too well, you haven't lost much. Often you'll find, as Ginger and I have, that your partner's response is positive and that your caution was unnecessary. A simple way to make intimacy easier is to talk about your fears and why it's hard to share them. That's being intimate. Besides, knowing why each of you fears being close should help you to be more patient with each other.

Give It Time

Getting close takes time. That's just the way it is. As a woman once told us, "Marriage is like being together, then pulled apart and then together again, then apart." Our relationship is more like a roller coaster of highs and lows than a steady, elevated ride on a monorail. After being away from each other for a while, it takes some warming up to get close. Joining physically might happen quickly, but bonding emotionally doesn't. Ginger and I learned this from what happened on our evenings out. Moments for just the two of us at home were scarce with our children around. To get time together, we scheduled a night out each week. How we would look forward to those dinners, picnics, or whatever it was that would get us face-to-face alone. Throughout the week we'd think of things to talk about then.

When the evening came, we would eagerly climb into our car expecting to ride full speed into blissful intimacy. Instead, we rode in silence. The dialogue was usually, "Don't you feel like talking?" "No, do you?" "No." "OK." And it was OK. We learned to be comfortable with silence, but that's not what we had in mind. Then, slowly, we would unfold as the evening did. Conversation would start with the salad or at least with the second cup of coffee. Into the meal, talk turned to children or finances.

Then we reminded ourselves that our evening was not planned to discuss these. Eventually we moved into more intimate areas—only after a while. Getting into each other's depths requires wading in the shallow parts first. Significant talk follows small talk, and that takes time.

Put Your Hearts into It

Sex will even be better when it takes place in an aura of closeness. Couples can deliberately try to combine their sexual times together with other forms of intimacy. You and your spouse can assemble you own repertoire of ways to link soulishly as you do sensually: reading love poems, listening to romantic music, sharing secret feelings and thoughts—all while in various states of undress or even in sexual embrace. Not that quickies are bad, since sometimes all we need and have time for is a swift romp to release our sexual tension. But the best sex is created like good soup, with the ingredients blended by simmering on low heat for a long time.

Embody It

While there are many highways to intimacy, let's not forget that physical lovemaking is one of them. We rightfully criticize people's tendency to sex-ualize intimacy in our society, particularly the men who do so. Yet we should realize that, as I mentioned in chapter 1, a person may want to make love in order to feel close. After explaining this, I have often had wives tell me, "I think I better understand my husband, especially one of the reasons he wants sex so often. I always thought it was just a physical thing with him. Now I see he may often want to get close to me—and that's the way he does it." It will make a difference in how we view our own desires and our partner's if we recognize that often behind craving for sex is a yearning for intimacy.

This insight should inspire us to make our sexual relationship a virtual freeway to intimacy. Being playfully creative, we can test techniques and variations by asking, "Does it make us feel close?" This is not the only cri-terion for judging what you include in your lovemaking; we'll mention others later. But the degree of intimacy is one of them, since sex offers us so many novel ways to foster feelings of closeness. That feeling is intensified by the fact that what happens in the bedroom is done in private. Known only to the two of you, they bind you together in a special pact of secrecy.

Hang Up the Hang-Ups

If we are to enrich our sex lives, we must deal with any personal hang-ups we have with intimacy. A middle-aged man once confided that in twenty years of marriage, he has rarely seen his wife naked. Before having sex with him, she undresses in the closet and then slips into bed in the darkness. Her reluctance to disrobe lies in a deep-seated fear of disclosing herself. She must deal with her personal problem in order to solve the sexual problem—depriving her husband of one of the delicacies of married life: the sight of a partner's body.

In this case this woman's problem was not with sex but with intimacy. The cause of such trouble usually lies in the past. Perhaps our parents bombarded us with phrases like "don't cry" or "don't feel sad," binding our emotions in a straitjacket of fear, guilt, and shame. Or we may have been reared in a dysfunctional family.

A former student of mine came to me for help after hearing me lecture about how our families shape us. Getting close to girls was a dilemma for this thirty-something young man. "I date frequently, hoping sometime to find someone to marry," he related. "But I can't stay in a relationship. Any time I get a little bit close to a girl, I drop her instantly—as simple as her taking my hand when crossing a street. That's it. We're history; I can't stand the thought of going further." He then told me that he grew up in the home of a drug addict. As a child, this young man was emotionally isolated and was made to spend many hours each week in opium dens while his father satisfied his addiction. As an adult, he can't tolerate intimacy because as a child he rarely experienced it.

Research confirms that families of abusers, alcoholics, and those addicted to drugs, gambling, sex, or even work create an aversion to intimacy. Feelings in these families are held hostage by three unspoken rules: "Don't trust; don't feel; don't talk." Shame keeps people from talking about the addict's behavior and the chaos it causes in the home. "It's like having an elephant in the living room," they say, "and no one mentions it's there." And no one is allowed to mention the anger, sadness, or hurt he or she may be feeling. As a result, family members don't communicate on an emotional level about much of anything.

Other types of childhood experiences, such as being rejected by a parent, also produce people who have trouble with intimacy. To avoid being hurt, these people learn to keep their distance from others. Sometimes that distancing is conscious, as is the case with Paula, who defines herself as a writer first and then a wife. Although she's a Christian and knows that her husband's needs matter, she also knows that success goes to those who avoid heavy relationships. Because she felt rejected as a child, she will never get so deeply involved as to be hurt that way again.

Still other people remain distant from their spouse without being conscious of why. Phil, who was rejected by his mentally ill mother, has built a hard shell around himself to keep from being hurt again. Fear of losing his autonomy keeps him from fully giving himself to his wife. Phil has convinced himself that marriage, sex, and intimacy are not important. Paula and Phil must first admit they have a problem if they are going to tackle it. Paula must rethink her priorities, recognizing that intimate abandonment in a one-flesh relationship is what God has called her to. Phil must recognize how his past has created his abnormal fear of intimacy and believe he can overcome it.

Sex therapists talk about people with the Madonna/prostitute complex—someone who can have sex with bad people but not with good ones. Associating sex with power, they are turned on by a partner who is inferior to themselves. Afraid of true intimacy, they cannot trust their spouse in a close relationship and therefore do not turn on to them sexually. Any kind of abandonment or abuse, especially incest, can produce this attitude. In incest situations the child usually cannot even trust the other parent; with no one to turn to, the child learns not to trust. In the words of one expert, the young victim had no safe harbor to go to. In some instances, incest may have made the child feel powerful, as when a father rewarded his daughter with privileges or gifts or made her feel special because of their sexual relationship. In the process, the child failed to learn other forms of intimacy and tied sex to power instead of closeness.

Being Christians should give us an advantage because we are to be dedicated to truth. Put off falsehood and speak truth to one another, said Paul. Of all people we should have nothing to hide and should face ourselves honestly. The church is the only organization I know that requires people to confess publicly that they are sinners as a requirement for membership.

We should be able to accept ourselves and others, faults and all, because Christ has accepted us (Rom. 15:7). Knowing this, we will try to foster a climate of warm acceptance in our marriage that will enable each other slowly to open, just as the petals of a rose unfold in the sunlight.

Be Lifetime Explorers

A man and wife should passionately want to know each other. "I see my wife as a vast forest, and I am an explorer," said one man. If the searching stops, the excitement ends; marriage becomes a bore.

A word of caution: We should not be too eager to learn too much, too soon of each other. Some things should never be revealed, and others only after a period of time. The Bible offers a good rule to follow: Say what will build others up (Eph. 4:29). That doesn't mean we might not have to say something that hurts, since it sometimes takes that to produce growth. The point is that being intimate doesn't demand sharing everything we think or feel. Kept secrets contribute to a relationship just as revealed ones do. Being a bit mysterious to each other is part of the wonder of a relationship. Even the most intimate couples will not be completely known to each other.

Through years of patient unfolding, a couple can create a relationship that truly deserves the title "intimate friends." Encounters of open, honest sexual abandon will build in intensity and meaning, each one warmed by the memories of all that has gone before.

~🦋 Pillow Talk 🦋~

AN INTIMACY INVENTORY

The theme of this chapter is that couples should cultivate many forms of intimacy. This Pillow Talk will help you know which types of intimacy you will want to develop more in your marriage.

First, each of you should evaluate your intimacy in each area by selecting a number that depicts how strong or weak you believe it is, with weak being a smaller number and strong being a higher number.

Second, share with each other to determine:

1. Your strong and weak areas.

2. Any areas that neither of you value as important to you as a couple.

3. Any areas that you both agree you should continue to pursue and even try to improve.

Sexual Intimacy   1 2 3 4 5 6

mutual sensual pleasuring and nearness as well as sharing expressions of passionate abandon

Intellectual Intimacy   1 2 3 4 5 6

discussing together opinions, ideas, beliefs, and values—meeting and interacting mind to mind

Aesthetic Intimacy   1 2 3 4 5 6

together encountering beauty in its many forms in God's creation or in human creative arts and activities

Creative Intimacy   1 2 3 4 5 6

sharing in creative acts, whether birthing children or cultivating a garden or decorating a room

Recreational Intimacy   1 2 3 4 5 6

participating together in leisure activities as spectators or participants

Work Intimacy   1 2 3 4 5 6

doing chores together, solving problems, making a living, or serving together in the community or the church

Crisis Intimacy   1 2 3 4 5 6

jointly facing life's difficulties and challenges and supporting each other through hard times

Commitment Intimacy   1 2 3 4 5 6

believing in and standing for the same beliefs, values, and other convictions

Spiritual Intimacy   1 2 3 4 5 6

being together with God, praying to, worshiping, learning about, or serving him

Emotional Intimacy   1 2 3 4 5 6

opening up to each other, disclosing private thoughts and deep feelings

Chapter Three

SEX AND PROCREATION
YOU WOULDN'T BE WITHOUT IT

*S*ex is OK; without it none of us would be here," preached Billy
Graham. After creating Adam and Eve, God gave his first command
to humanity: "Be fruitful and increase in number; fill the earth and subdue it" (Gen. 1:28). And to obey him they would need to make love.
Reproduction is the most obvious purpose of our sexuality, one that has
major implications for how we view and practice sex. Most obvious is that
we should respect it. Anyone who has looked into the eyes of a cooing
baby has had to admit that the process that produced something so
lovable has to be good as well. How could it be otherwise?

Even past Christian leaders who taught that sex is dirty and disgusting grudgingly permitted it in marriage for producing children. It's too
bad they didn't see how having children could make lovemaking special.
Recently, at a dinner with our four children, their spouses, and our eight
grandchildren, Ginger looked at them and said, "Isn't it amazing; all of this
because I said 'I do.'" I thought but didn't say, "And also because you, on
many occasions, said yes." That our relationship has produced such
wonderful children has, for us, put a halo around it.

Being a part of each parent, a baby is the visible expression of two
people having become one flesh. Our natural children should make us
cherish the bodies that produced them. Stretch marks, pudginess, and
other effects of childbearing ought to increase a husband's admiration for

his wife. This appreciation is especially crucial as a couple grows older and the wear and tear of rearing children takes its toll on both of them. Unfortunately, we are losing sight of this value; as a society, we have gone from the idea of sex only for having children to the idea of sex for anything but. Not that childbearing is the only bond or the only meaning given to a couple's love life, although for some people it seems to be. A friend of mine confided that the only time his wife has been sexually responsive was when they were trying to have children. Apparently her arousal mechanism is tied to having sex to have babies.

INCONCEIVABLE ISSUES

If this woman's attitude is the right one to have, it raises all sorts of questions. Is having sex justified when conception isn't possible—for infertile couples, for those beyond childbearing age, or during pregnancy? Is it right to use birth control techniques to prevent conception? Is sexual intercourse the only way a couple should climax, since it fits the procreative purpose of their lovemaking?

Currently not all of these are pressing questions among Christians. But birth control is still an issue for many people; and other issues, though they are not often discussed, may trouble other people. All of these questions have been dealt with in the past, often in a surprisingly frank way. Seeing how they were handled then may help us think more clearly about them now.

For centuries, especially during the Middle Ages, church leaders judged all marital sex by its reproductive purpose. Any sensual activity was morally right only if it was tied to conceiving a child. Anal intercourse, for example, was wrong because it didn't fit this criterion. So were certain positions: the woman being on top, for instance, was considered "against nature" because she was more likely to retain the seed if she were underneath.[1]

Some church fathers "taught that sexual intercourse was forbidden when a man's wife was already pregnant. It was regarded as unreasonable to sow seed in a field that had already been planted."[2] The emphasis in these situations was on the couple's intention which is how they were able to justify sex when conception was not possible, as with infertile couples or older people. In these cases it was argued that sex at these times was acceptable because the couple were not giving up their intention to conceive, which was the real issue.[3]

Christian theologians today do not judge all sexual behavior by its reproductive role. Since they believe sex has other purposes, avoiding conception in order to fulfill them is acceptable. Roman Catholics as well as Protestants believe there are biblically based purposes for sex other than conceiving babies; thus it is right to have sex even when the intent is not to conceive. Otherwise, infertile couples would have no reason to make love, nor would couples who are past the age of childbearing. What the Roman Catholic Church objects to is not family planning but the use of artificial means to do so. Couples may use the rhythm method—having sex when a wife is least likely to conceive—but they should always permit the possibility of conception to take place. Protestants take issue with this view, believing that the use of contraceptives is an exercise of control over our lives that God has granted us. Relying on the phrase "fill the earth and subdue it" (Gen. 1:28), they maintain we may use our God-given intellectual powers to regulate our lives, including responsible planning of our family.

Besides choosing a method that is convenient, reliable, and safe, there is one other matter to consider when you consult your doctor for advice: the ethics of abortion. Those of us who are pro-life caution couples to select a method that prevents conception, not one that can cause abortion. Certain devices, in addition to physician-assisted abortion, act in this way.

The Childish Decision for Grown-Ups

Couples who are thinking about having children should ask why they might want to. It's possible to want to have children for the wrong reasons, just as it is to decide not to have them for the wrong reasons. Authors of *The Parent Test* give four helpful categories for examining motives for having children.

Egotistic reasons include having a child who will look like the parent(s) or who will carry on one's admirable traits. Other such reasons are having a child who will be successful or will carry on a family name. Still other reasons include "to feel the pride of creating," "to keep me young in heart," or "to help me feel fulfilled."

Compensatory motives are to be like most people, to please one's parents, or to forestall social criticism. These are not as dangerous as the preceding ones, but they are still poor reasons for becoming parents.

Affectionate motives are "to have a real opportunity to make someone happy," "to teach someone about all the beautiful things of life," "to have the satisfaction of giving myself to someone else," or "to help someone grow and develop." These are good reasons for wanting to parent a child.

The blessings of birth. Though you'll want to have affectionate reasons, you'll also probably decide to have a baby because of the rewards. The psalmist sang, "Behold, children are a gift of the LORD, the fruit of the womb is a reward" (Ps. 127:3 NASB).[4]

Much of the reward is in the experience itself. Parenting is participating in God's creative work. Women have a natural baby hunger; some of their creative powers are linked to their reproductive systems. "A woman giving birth to a child has pain because her time has come," observed Jesus, "but when her baby is born she forgets the anguish because of her joy that a child is born into the world" (John 16:21).

Ninety percent of the motivation for becoming a parent is embedded in the heart of a husband or a wife. At the same time, arguments against having children pile up: they're too much work and too expensive; the times are too depressing; we aren't sure if we'll make good parents. The tension over whether to conceive is great. "Most often a couple will decide that they are simply doing what seems natural in God's plan for His creation."[5] And their role in that plan should make them value each other as well as the passionate love that is part of the process.

THE EMBODIMENT OF LOVE

The procreative purpose of sex should make us think about it in another way: that it is a physical process. To keep our love life humming, we need to understand each other's and our own sexuality. All sorts of body functions and parts are involved: genitals, glands, hormones, blood vessels, body chemistry. If these aren't functioning properly, no amount of love or intention will make someone a passionate lover. It's wrong to say to someone, "You don't love me because you don't want me." The lack of desire may be more a matter of the body than of the heart. You need to know that fact in order to deal with it. The same is true of other sexual dysfunctions. To fix them you'll need to learn as much as you can about how male and female bodies work.

Let's look at the physical aspects of the three stages of sex. Sex drive is the first stage, and not everything is known about how our bodies contribute to our sensual desires. We know our bodies need to be rested and have a certain measure of health; stress and fatigue are two major killers of libido. To crave each other, we sometimes need a restful evening more than we do a romantic one. Tiredness and tension can reduce our ardor for long periods of time and during certain times of life, and these are ever-present realities. "A woman at 40 is usually responsible for a huge number of roles: taking care of a home and kids, working, maybe volunteer work, too," says psychologist Nancy Molitor, program director of the Center for Women's Behavioral Health at Evanston Northwestern Health Care. "It is certainly a factor in limiting her libido."

At some times in our lives, the frequency of sexual intimacy may drop from once or twice a week to every other week, even once a month. Frequency may also determine desire. Ironically, the less sex a couple has, the less they want—thus the saying "use it or lose it." That's because intercourse prompts the release of a "desire hormone," Molitor says. "The more sex you have, the more you release this hormone."[6] The number of times has a limit, of course, since everyone needs some time to recharge. Some experts claim that demanding too much sex, especially from a wife, can lead to sexual anorexia.[7] It's better to wait until your partner is not just ready but eager.

Sexual appetite is also altered by certain diseases: diabetes, heart and circulatory problems, and the like. Medicine can even play a role; certain prescription drugs act like a cold shower. For both men and women, hormones are craving regulators. For this reason menopause and aging may contribute to a decreasing interest in sex. However, research shows that after menopause, most women say their sexual fervor continues, many reporting that it increases. And scientists claim that the same is true of middle-aged men. Aging may take a toll on some, but seniors—including those in their eighties and nineties—report their libido is not deserving of an obituary.

A woman's level of eagerness will fluctuate with her menstrual cycle, since body chemistry plays a role in sexual desire and hers is constantly changing. Ardor reaches a peak two times a month: in the middle of the cycle, when the egg drops, and then a few days before menstruation. Watching the calendar will not only clue a husband about when to try to get his wife in the mood, it will make it easier for her to let him. And, if they want to drive each other over the edge, they will both know when it's most likely to happen.

The intricacies of a woman's sexual desire are more complex than a man's and are still a mystery. Her drives are more a matter of heart than body. That the average woman's sexual peak is in her early thirties, versus a man's in his late teens, seems to confirm this. A young wife appears to need years of bonding with her husband before her sex drive gets into high gear. But the study of female sexuality, which has accelerated in the last few years, promises to offer some physiological solutions to these mysteries.

To date, medical research and treatment focus on the two other stages of sex—arousal and orgasm. One such treatment for a low threshold of arousal, Viagra, is a remedy for penile dysfunction. To be erect, the penis needs more blood flowing into it than goes out, and for various reasons, some men don't have enough blood flow to make that happen. Viagra arouses the man by increasing the flow.

By contrast, Viagra has not been very effective in getting women to higher levels of passion. A woman's genitals engorge with blood during arousal, and researchers had hoped that Viagra would relax the tissue in a woman's clitoris, allowing the vessels in the organ to swell with blood. Although Viagra has not produced this effect in women, the EROS-CTD, a clitoris suction-cup device, is now for sale. This device is about the size of a computer mouse and draws blood to the clitoris.

Herbs and drugs are used to treat people with low sex desire and problems with arousal. But one expert claims that these substances are physically useless, and according to a recent *Newsweek* report, most of these aphrodisiacs probably will not produce the desired results. There is some promise, however; men with impotence caused by diabetes can get help from a prescription drug derived from a compound in the bark of the African yohimbe tree. As yet there are no FDA-approved herbs that increase libido for women.[8]

The same seems to be true for orgasm, the third sexual stage. Treatments that enhance men's arousal contribute to orgasm for men and thus for their wives, who benefit from their husbands' restored ability. For women, too, anything that helps them get aroused will also help them have an orgasm, since both arousal and orgasm are related to the blood flow to the genitals. During orgasm, muscle contractions force blood from the genitals, so any treatment that helps engorge this area will also help a woman reach a climax.

Though medical science doesn't have cures for all sexual dysfunctions or doesn't provide proven helps to enhance a couple's sex life, we owe it to ourselves and especially our partners to consider the physical dimensions of our sexuality and consult a doctor or sex therapist when necessary. Sex is a two-step process; it involves the physical capacity for it as well as healthy thoughts and attitudes toward it. Thus we should learn all we can about sex as a biological process, as God created it. At the same time we should recognize that the context of sex is far more important than the physiology. In a letter to the editors of *Newsweek,* one woman joked that Viagra could help women's sexual functioning if it increased the flow of blood to men's ears. And we should know how physical factors affect our sensual relationship and then do something about them. The best foreplay, for instance, may mean a husband watches the children while his wife takes a badly needed nap.

Experts especially warn couples to be cautious about how they react if a woman is unable to have orgasms or does so with great difficulty. Couples tend to turn this into a greater problem than it is. They, especially the husband, will become greatly disturbed by her lack and try so hard to have orgasms that it creates conflict between them. They should understand that some wives are content to be without the majesty of the big O, finding satisfaction and pleasure in physically connecting with their husbands. And they should realize that difficulties with orgasm during the early period of marriage will often disappear later.

Certainly couples should not neglect the clitoris, the primary trigger of an orgasm. And, though many of them are, they should not be embarrassed to use a vibrator for the added stimulation some women need. Many Christian sex therapists also counsel a nonorgasmic woman to practice bringing herself to a climax. Since there is no biblical injunction against masturbation, she should feel no guilt if she masturbates, especially since her goal is to become a better sexual partner to her husband. Whatever good comes from her solo times is easily transferred to her duet with her husband.

SEXUAL INTERCOURSE IS GENDER INTERCOURSE

Since God created sex as a biological process involving males and females, it's crucial that each gender understand the other, especially how they differ. Both their pleasures with each other and their problems come from these amazing, somewhat mystical, differences. Much has been made of the dissimilarities of men and women and the resulting failure of each to understand the other. But if we are unsolved mysteries to each other, it is not because no one has studied the differences. We are awash in research data that explain what they are.

It's not always politically correct to focus on our differences because doing so sometimes results in demeaning women. Feminists rightly feared that research showed females were different from males would be used to claim women were inferior to men. However, I believe we are getting beyond making such unfair judgments and are realizing the strength and importance of both feminine and masculine traits. Christians especially should value each gender equally because we believe the differences between them were created by God.

Anatomical Differences

Beyond the obvious differences, men and women are anatomically distinct in scores of ways that shape their behavior. Men have a higher metabolic rate than women, and they convert more energy to muscle; women store more of it into fat. Males, on the average, have denser, stronger bones, tendons, and ligaments. This strength, along with their body's ability to create energy, allows them to do heavier work and perform better in sports that require short bursts of strength. Women, however, do better in activities that require endurance; they equal the performance of men in long-distance swimming and running. This is because their thicker layer of subcutaneous fat gives them a better energy supply than men have.

Because their bodies favor fat storage, women have trouble eating enough to get the vitamins they need without adding fat. However troubling it is to them, this extra fat may be useful in bearing children, since they may need a certain level of fat to carry the fetus and to provide milk after birth. Excessively thin women have more trouble conceiving children than do other women, causing some scientists to speculate that the cultural emphasis on thinness may contribute to today's high levels of infertility.[9]

Men generally are more active and more prone to take risks than are women. Many anatomical factors are behind this. Men have larger windpipes and 30 percent greater lung capacity than females do. Men's blood has more red blood cells and thus can carry more oxygen than a woman's. Add to this their relatively larger heart, fewer sensory nerve endings in the skin, and higher peripheral pain tolerance. All of these physical differences may be what make men so aggressive when they make love.

Limbic System Differences

Readiness for sex is one of the most obvious areas in which males and females differ. A wife soon learns, if she hadn't already read about it, that a man can be aroused quickly, igniting like a pile of dry leaves. She, as her husband soon learns, is more like a stack of charcoal briquettes, slow to catch fire, though eventually able to reach the same degree of heat.

These different reaction times are partly due to something you probably haven't noticed: your spouse's limbic system operates differently from your own. The limbic system is the seat of our drives and emotions—hunger, thirst, sex, fighting, fleeing—and it continually shifts our attention from one drive to another. When there is enough stimulation in the hypothalamus, which is located in the brain, we act. Then once drives are satisfied, the hypothalamus stimulates the pleasure center.[10]

Stimulation, however, is not the same for males and females. In men, testosterone stimulates the production of a neurotransmitter in the hypothalamic area. In women, estrogen has the opposite effect, inhibiting synaptic firings. The result is this: Men's drives are set off by less stimulation than it takes to set off women's drives. This could explain why females may be more patient with children, who can provide plenty of stimulation to the limbic system. It also may explain why, when it comes to getting hot, men are the microwave; women, the oven.

Differences in Triggers of Arousal

Generally, facets of a personal relationship arouse a woman. Her readiness for intercourse is tied to how she feels about a man as a person. This may be due to the role she plays in conceiving a child. Because sexual intercourse could make her pregnant, she may be more cautious about it, as well as with whom she has intercourse. Her body is threatened in a way a man's isn't. As someone has said, "Sex for a man may last nine minutes; for a woman it could last nine months." Since contraceptives have reduced the threat of pregnancy, women's behavior is changing. Studies show that women have become more promiscuous than they were in the past, and things more overtly sexual seem to play more of a role in turning them on. Yet research also confirms that for women a personal relationship is still the most important gateway to a sexual one. A woman responds to commitment, kindness, love, and all the other qualities that would make her feel safe to bear a child with a man. Most women see sex in terms of a total relationship. Perhaps the position of her genitals also contributes to this: she receives the man into her body and seemingly participates in sex more wholly than he does.

A man's sexual triggers are not so holistic. Personal elements do not figure as highly in his arousal mechanism because he is turned on by his eyes more than by his heart. Though a man does love a woman for her personality, it is the sight of her body that arouses him. As Swedish reformer Ellen Key so eloquently said, "With women love usually proceeds from the soul to the senses and sometimes does not reach so far . . . with man it usually proceeds from the senses to the soul and sometimes never completes the journey."

Because arousal is not the same for men and women, couples need to take this into account. It's up to the man to compensate for this difference—a woman can't make her body speed up, but he can make his slow down. Yet many men fail to do this. In surveys, interviews, and counseling situations, wives still complain that their husbands do not give much forethought to foreplay despite all that has been written about it. Many of the suggestions in this book will help a man because most of these suggestions focus on the personal side of marriage and sex that women especially value. A wise husband knows that giving his wife a gentle, warm kiss in the morning can lead to a passionate time with her in the evening.

A man not only needs to slow down his approach to getting his wife in bed but also to put on the brakes after he gets her there. He can learn to drive her wild, but not at breakneck speeds. He must adjust to her low speed limit. For most men, whose tendency is to hurry, this will take some patience and bedroom education. Doing what comes naturally will not work in this case. If a wife and husband did that, he would have crossed the finish line before she started her engine.

Other chapters in this book, as well as in a good sex manual, will give a man plenty of ideas on how to slow down. Essentially, he needs to do relational things along with the sexual—listen to music, watch a video, or read love poems after getting started. Then focus on nongenital contact, giving each other sensual pleasure that avoids the most sensitive spots. Pleasuring his wife on various parts of her body with his hands and mouth can rev her up and keep him on idle. After joining, keep going by varying the pace and changing positions. Disconnect, too, and go back to other types of pleasuring.

Blessed is the man who can adjust to his wife's sensual pace. Not only will she be grateful to him, but also he will be erotically rewarded. Years of patient efforts to rouse her to sensual heights will pay off in another way: she eventually will become more like him. Research shows that in midlife, men and women become more alike. In serious relations after age thirty-five, wives get more erotic and become aroused more quickly. Men in turn come to appreciate more intimacy, love, and other facets of the second language of sex.[11] In fact, it was also discovered that after age forty-five, women are more physically motivated for sex than men are. The poet Robert Browning knew what he was talking about when he wrote, "Grow old along with me, the best is yet to be."

Another gender difference is bound to show up under the covers. After climaxing, a wife typically wants to linger in her husband's arms, reveling in her slowly fading passion. She can't understand why he jumps out of bed, races downstairs to make a ham sandwich and watch a late-night movie. Perhaps she accuses him of being interested only in his own satisfaction. However, she needs to realize that his after-sex reaction has a physical cause. When he climaxed, he emptied numerous glands throughout his body. For him orgasm shut down his engine as promptly as turning off the ignition in a car. His attention quickly turns to something other than his wife's body. She may not fully comprehend this because, even after orgasm, her engine continues to idle. A little understanding can resolve any tension this may create. She can realize his sudden disinterest in her is physiological, not emotional. And he can linger with her, allowing her afterglow to dim slowly while she's in his arms.

The Brain: Differences in Perception and Sensitivities

Even the body hair of each gender may play a role in your love life. A woman's hair is finer and is more easily moved than a man's, so she has a finer sense perception. Besides this, a woman's skin is more sensitive to touch than a man's. This may be why women like gentle stroking, especially during the early stages of lovemaking.[12] This can conflict with a man's tendency to get too rough too soon, his aggression being fueled by that robust hormone, testosterone.

And what about those nights when, in the middle of lovemaking, a woman hears something outside the bedroom that quickly diverts her attention? His concentration firmly fixed on sex, her husband accuses her of hearing things. She counters by claiming that the hearing problem is his, not hers. They are probably both right. She hears things he doesn't because a woman's hearing, on average, is better than a man's. So are her senses of smell and taste. In contrast, a man's power of concentration on what he's doing is such that it would seem he could have sex anywhere, anytime—in a tent, in the middle of a thunderstorm. His wife's concentration, to his dismay, is not so sharp.

Women are usually more perceptive and aware of their surroundings than are men, and this difference also shows up in the bedroom. I once counseled newlyweds who reaped the harvest of this difference in the middle of their honeymoon. The wife wasn't showing much exuberance during their initial lovemaking sessions. Wedded bliss was wedded dull, according to him. He couldn't understand why she couldn't see that camping in the mountains, making loving in a tent, was the most romantic setting newlyweds could have. For years he had dreamed of such a honeymoon. To her his dream was a nightmare; this, her first camping trip, was uncomfortable, scary, and definitely not conducive to cleanliness. While he was dreamily thinking of sex, she was wistfully pondering a shower.

Context played a major role in lovemaking for her, as it does for women in general. I explained this to him, reassuring him that his wife's eroticism was not in question. In fact, when I asked if she had displayed any passion since the wedding, they explained that she had—the night they stayed in a motel. He readily accepted the solution to the mystery his wife already knew and promised to buy, posthaste, a sex manual that would help him understand his wife. Apparently, his B.A. degree didn't prepare him for his role as a husband. (Is that why they call it a bachelor's degree?)

This power of concentration (his) or this power of distraction (hers) may be in their heads. For some time, scientists have known that the brains of men and women are not exactly the same, the difference being in the *corpus callosum*. In this bridge between the right and left hemispheres, women have more fibers. This better connection enables women to access both hemispheres at the same time, while men tend to isolate functions of one side or the other.

Because the right side of the brain tends to view things more holistically, this causes women to allow their keen sense of their surroundings to interrupt their left-brain concentration, much as a ham operator's radio signal breaks in on an FM station. This static then interferes with the sensual music a woman and her husband are making, and for the moment, she turns it off, much to his dismay and confusion.

But her awareness of context can be a turn-on as well as a turn-off. This is why I once advised a couple to do something about their bedroom. He, like the outdoorsman, complained that his wife was not spirited in the bedroom. She explained, "Though I love my husband and want to be sensual, our bedroom is not something to get turned on about." She then described a room with a wall-to-wall bed and only the barest of furniture and decorations. Besides, a naked lightbulb hung on an electric cord from the ceiling. "When I lie there having sex, staring up at that bare light, I feel like a prostitute in a seedy hotel," she said.

Before our session was over, they decided that though their income was limited and they couldn't afford a bedroom that made her feel like a queen, they could create one that would make her feel like a respectable woman. Creating a sensual, romantic ambience in the bedroom is a good plan for any couple. Even an inexpensive colored lightbulb in a lamp can do wonders.

This feminine ability to pick up clues from her surroundings may account for a wife's sensitivity to her husband's moods. She has more ability to read faces than he has. She can pick up subtle signs of his anger, sadness, or disappointment. And she will probably ask him to reassure her that he is not upset with her. Because of her greater concern for a total relationship, she may be reluctant to make love unless he convinces her nothing's wrong. This may help explain how men and women relate sex to marital conflict. After a fight, men want to make love to make up. Women want to make up before making out.

All of this is because we have different brains. We need to use them to recognize that God has made humanity diverse: male and female. A man recently told me that reading a book on how women think has revolutionized his marriage. Any husband and wife who accept their differences and adjust to them will do the same. Though our gender differences sometimes cause conflict in the bedroom, they create the ecstasy there as well. Let's celebrate them.

~ *Pillow Talk* ~

SEEING THE DIFFERENCE OUR DIFFERENCES MAKE

This chapter has described a number of differences between men and women and the roles they may play in a couple's love life. The purpose of this Pillow Talk is to stimulate you to discuss and deal with how you and your partner are different.

First, using the following list of differences mentioned in the chapter, decide which apply to you as a couple. Then try to determine how each difference affects your relationship, both positively and negatively.

1. Men are more inclined to be risk takers than are women.

2. Men are more aggressive than women in making love.

3. In general, men's drives and emotions—such as hunger, thirst, sex, fighting, and fleeing—are set off by less stimulation than it takes for women.

4. When it comes to being sexually aroused, women are like ovens; men are like microwaves.

5. Women are more patient than men are.

6. Women are sensually aroused by relational factors; men, by physical ones.

7. Men are more turned on by what they see than are women.

8. After climaxing, a woman's passion subsides more slowly than a man's does.

9. In general, a woman's greater sensitivity to touch makes her want gentler stroking than a man wants.

10. A woman's hearing is better than a man's.

11. During lovemaking a man's concentration is intense; a woman may be more easily distracted.

12. A woman is more sensitive to her surroundings when having sex than is a man.

13. A woman is more sensitive to her husband's moods than he is to hers.

14. In midlife, husbands and wives become more alike in their motivation for sex—she being more interested in the physical; he, the relational. (Is this true for you yet?)

15. Other differences not mentioned?

Chapter Four

SEX AND LOVE

LOVE IS MORE THAN A FOUR-LETTER WORD

*R*omantic love is as American as apple pie and the Fourth of July. Even preschool children know what it is. Fairy tales such as "Beauty and the Beast," "Cinderella," and "Sleeping Beauty" indoctrinate them with the boy-meets-girl theme. They expect to fall in love, like the princes and princesses, and live happily ever after. Pop songs and romance novels continue to inspire their fantasies of being deeply in love forever. Yet childhood fantasies do not always turn into adult realities. In marriages sometimes the prince turns into a beast, to the dismay of many women. And Sleeping Beauty is not always aroused by a kiss, to the disappointment of many men. Disillusioned, many couples have abandoned any hope of romance continuing in their marriage.

ROMANTIC LOVE LIKE CHEWING GUM

Perhaps, they're right. After all, romantic love causes a lot of heartache. People madly in love often end up being shunned, jilted, or otherwise hurt. These potentially agonizing results from falling in love make many people feel it's an illusion they can't afford to keep.

This contempt and indifference was especially true before our modern era. Three hundred years ago a physician designated romantic love a disease, claiming that lightning, wars, fires, and plagues have not done as much mischief to mankind as what he called "this brutish passion."

Though today we have a healthier view of this savage emotion, we tend not to expect it to last long in a marriage. Social scientists tell us it won't last long after the wedding, fading after about two or three years, or even months. Like a piece of gum, the flavor doesn't last. In its place grows what some have called "companionate love," a more mature sort. We feel that we just can't expect the degree of novelty, excitement, and ecstasy of early marriage to continue. The blush of first love seems too hot a level to maintain in the cold climate of marriage. Cool is mature. Love, like a developing insect, needs to metamorphose into something more stable and grown-up. Passionate love gives way to companionship love, a lower-key feeling of friendly affection and attachment. Here's how one woman describes the journey from passion to companionship:

When I fell in love, I felt fantastic! I glowed, people said they never saw me prettier or happier. . . . As it turned out, I married Ted. We're still very happy and very much in love, but there is a definite difference between the first passionate feelings of love and the now mellowed out. Don't get me wrong, though, there are still plenty of passionate times. It's just that when you live together, the passion is not as urgent a thing. You're more loving friends.[1]

Something's puzzling about this point of view. Most couples expect their love to last, yet they're supposed to think it will mutate into something different. If it turns into a feeling of companionship, is it still the same love? Should we exchange our dream of being passionate lovers for being loving friends?

Before we tackle these questions, I need to offer a definition of romantic love, since there are many different ideas about it. I like the definition by Nathaniel Branden, who describes it as "a passionate spiritual-emotional-sexual attachment between a man and woman that reflects a high regard for the value of each other's person."[2] Note that for him, love has to be intense and sensual, with strong mutual admiration and concern—a feeling of being soul mates. Unlike some social scientists, Branden believes such love can be sustained in a marriage. He describes the love he and his wife of fifteen years had for each other:

On the morning of that day [the day of her accidental death] we lingered in bed, making love and talking about the excitement we felt in each other's presence, an excitement like no other in our lives, that seemed almost magically and irresistibly self-rejuvenating. When Patrecia entered the room, the lights of my world got brighter.[3]

As Christians, we can turn to the Scriptures for answers to our questions about romantic love. And to do so, we will need to examine the whole biblical picture of human love and especially compare and contrast it with popular views of romantic love.

THE DIVINE PORTRAIT OF LOVE

One dramatic portrait of human love is found in chapter 5 of Paul's letter to the Ephesians. For two thousand years, biblical scholars and theologians have recognized this and have scrutinized this passage to make sense of Christian love. In verse 25, Paul commands husbands to love their wives as "Christ loved the church and gave himself up for her." This comparison with Christ's love for the church gave marriage a sacred tint, even for people who had little practical use for it.

Paul's idea of comparing God's love with marital love was not new; the comparison appears in the Old Testament as well.

By making this comparison, Paul sets God's love as the standard for any loving relationship. He commands all Christians: "Be imitators of God, therefore, as dearly loved children and live a life of love, just as Christ loved us and gave himself up for us as a fragrant offering and sacrifice to God" (Eph. 5:1–2). Husbands are to love their wives as Christ loves his people, the church. Wives should love their husbands in this same way. Paul later makes a special application of this command to men, who are to love as Christ in a variety of ways.

Love's Loyalty

Faithfulness was a major feature of God's love in the Old Testament and also of Christ's love for his church, as the verse from Isaiah suggests: "Though the mountains be shaken and the hills be removed, yet my unfailing love for you will not be shaken" (54:10).

Love is to be loyal, claims Paul, because the husband and wife are "one flesh," just as Christ and the church are one. He quotes Genesis 2:24 to establish this fact: "We are members of his body. 'For this reason a man will leave his father and mother and be united to his wife, and the two will become one flesh.' This is a profound mystery—but I am talking about Christ and the church" (Eph. 5:30–32). Christ is one with the church because he loves it, but he also loves it because he is one with it. The same is true for a husband. "In the same way, husbands ought to love their wives as their own bodies" (Eph. 5:28). By this Paul is not saying that a man's self-love should be a pattern for loving his wife. Rather, since Christ's love is the model of his love, a man's wife is also his body, since he is one with her in marriage. Thus Paul reasons, "He who loves his wife loves himself."

When Jesus was asked about divorce, he spoke mostly about marriage. "Haven't you read . . . that at the beginning the Creator 'made them male and female,' and said, 'For this reason a man will leave his father and mother and be united to his wife, and the two will become one flesh'? So they are no longer two, but one" (Matt. 19:4–6). One of the marriage bonds is wrapped up in the phrase "be united." Essentially this means "to be joined to" or "to cling to."

Joining to a wife is an obvious reference to the sexual embrace with its interlocking of bodies. But being united means more than this. The Hebrew word is also used when speaking of the loyalty that exists between individuals. Often this word is used to describe people's clinging to God when others were abandoning him. Thus Moses says, "But all of you who held fast to the LORD your God are still alive today" (Deut. 4:4). Loving partners will hold fast to each other; they will be faithful.

What "Commit Meant"?

Loyalty to your partner demands more than avoiding an affair with another; it requires having an affair with your spouse. Most of us will never commit adultery, but we will be unfaithful; it's not a sin of commission but of omission. This commitment is personal. You are not just giving your time, energy, and resources. Marriage demands the offering of yourself— your body, your private and inner secrets in the most intimate union known to humans.

A story is told of a rich man who was testing his wife's loyalty. "Would you love me if I lost all my money?" he asked. "Yes, I would," she replied without hesitation. "I didn't marry you for your wealth." Testing her further, he asked, "Would you love me if I lost my hearing and became deaf?" "Yes," she replied. "What about if I became blind as well?" Growing a bit weary, she once again replied, "I would love you." Then he offered his final test: "Would you love me if I lost my mind and became insane?" At this she paused, carefully weighing her answer. "Who could love a penniless, deaf, blind idiot?" she answered. "But," she went on, "I'd take care of you." This personal commitment provides a firm psychological mattress under both spouses.

But even beyond being personal, a marital pledge is also social. Marriage is to be a publicly proclaimed act. When a man left his father and mother to be united to his wife, he did so in the sight of others. From the earliest times this was true for the Hebrews; at least both families of the couple witnessed their pledge of loyalty. Countless spiritual and social laws regulated the relationship, which therefore had to be public. Two of the Ten Commandments refer to marriage: adultery was to be punished, and men were ordered not even to covet their neighbors' wives. Society has a stake in marriage because stable marriages contribute to a stable society. There are enormous emotional, relational, and financial costs to the breakup of families.

Jesus adds another dimension to the commitment—the divine sanction: "Therefore what God has joined together, let man not separate" (Matt. 19:6). God, along with others, is a witness to your pledges. He created the marriage arrangement; when two people marry, it is as if he himself has joined them. Proverbs 2:17 refers to this divine sanction as well as the personal. The woman had left the partner of her youth; that is, she betrayed her husband. And she had forsaken the covenant made before God, no doubt a reference to her wedding vows made in God's presence.

A Christian minister once confided to a group of us that he felt badly that at times it was the fear of God that kept him from being unfaithful to his wife. He lamented that his loyalty to his wife wasn't enough for him to resist temptation. Yet I would judge that he is no different from the rest of us. Sometimes we need the threat of shame and guilt to keep us loyal during the rough spots of our marital relationship.

This fact need not put us under undue pressure. We know from Scripture that divorce and annulments are allowed for extreme cases. Rather, when you both realize that God has joined you together, it adds a needed sense of permanence. Granted, it forces you to a solid commitment, but it also assures you of your partner's full loyalty to you. Imagine how much anxiety you are spared. Can you envision what it would be like to wake up every morning wondering if your partner will continue to live with you?

When a Long-Term Bond Is a Good Investment

Being dedicated to a lifelong relationship can do a lot for your sex life, though many people think otherwise. Popular culture tends to glamorize short-term relationships, picturing the erotic delights of novelty over and against the dullness of familiarity. Yet time can do to love what it does to wine; a long-term relationship can result in a quality of love that poets long have celebrated.

Lovemaking after many years has a richness that novelty cannot have. Each session is like being at a campfire after having been at many campfires before. You bring to it the memories, conscious and unconscious, of all those that went before.

People who are committed have security as a context for their quarreling. Without it, they might fear facing conflict lest it drive their partner away. Their devotion is not based on the fickle impulses of romantic love but is rooted in the will. This means we can handle the fluctuations of our emotions and openly deal with our disagreements over sex and other issues. As one woman wrote in a note to her husband, "Jim, I hate you for what you did today. Love, Jane."

Commitment is a turn-on, at least for women. This probably explains why some women say that praying with their husbands sometimes arouses them. Women usually need intimacy and security to make them comfortable with sex, and praying with a husband seems to provide both. Praying out loud is intimate and a sign that a man is godly and will keep his commitment to his wife. Perhaps prayer is the aphrodisiac so many people have been looking for.

Partners who make a lifelong commitment also have a strong sense of belongingness that is at the heart of lovemaking. "I am my beloved's, and my beloved is mine," declares the woman in the Song of Songs (6:3 KJV).

Without a pledge of loyalty, this feeling is impossible. Otherwise it would be "my beloved is mine—for this week, at least."

Sex—More Blessed to Give Than to Receive?

Yet such love will require sacrifice, for Christ's dying for the church is at the heart of his love. So Paul urges husbands, "Love your wives as Christ loved the church and gave himself for her." Love is not always convenient and easy. It offers pain as well as pleasure. Often in marriage we will be asked to give when there may be little receiving. During times of stress or sickness, one partner may ask more of the other than he or she can give in return.

This contrasts with what we often think of as romantic love, which focuses more on getting than giving. People in love usually need someone to respond to them, to love them back. It's much like a tennis game; if you hit the ball over the net and the other person doesn't return it, there's no game. Romantic love is reciprocal. This is not to say that it is unwilling to sacrifice or that Christlike love involves only sacrifice. Romantics often do sacrificial things for each other, even dying for each other. And while our Lord gave himself for us, he receives in return our love for him. Yet giving is at the core of his love and of the love we should have for others. The apostle Paul graphically explained what it involves in his down-to-earth description in 1 Corinthians 13.

"Love is patient" (v. 4). When your spouse provokes you, you wait and then handle the dispute calmly at another time. You don't rush your spouse into growth or change. Like a gardener, you watch the other mature and blossom—with patience. Adjusting in the bedroom takes a lot of waiting on each other.

"Love is kind" (v. 4). While patience keeps us from making a nasty reaction, kindness causes us to make a positive one. Kindness reaches out to help and affirm others at any time. To be a good husband, Ernest Hemingway advised, men should be kind to their wives when they least deserve it because that's when they need it the most. That's good advice for anyone because all of us need someone to be nice when we're being ornery. This sort of kindness will serve us well in the bedroom. A wife wants a lover who is gentle and understanding, interested in meeting her need for personal closeness, not just in gratifying himself. A man needs a wife who graciously satisfies his sexual needs even though he may not have done much to merit it.

"Love . . . does not envy" (v. 4). There is no mental uneasiness over the other's success. There's no sulking because our partner is experiencing something we were denied. Being jealously competitive with each other will douse a couple's sexual desire. In fact, envy sometimes is the cause of wife abuse. Some men get angry when their wife's achievements seem to eclipse theirs, and they lash out.

"Love . . . does not boast, . . . is not proud" (v. 4). It's tough to live with a proud person. Love doesn't say, "Don't you know who I am? I deserve better than this." Humble lovers are grateful for what they receive. They don't try to prove themselves in bed, insisting their partner applaud their performance. Instead of saying, "Was it good for you?" they say, "I really enjoyed that."

"Love is not rude" (v. 5). Too often we reserve our politeness for people outside the family. We suppose we have the liberty to be harsh and brutally frank with those we're close to. Not so, says Paul. Love doesn't crudely criticize a partner who isn't making love as we would like. Instead of brusquely accusing, "What's wrong with you?" it asks respectfully, "Will you try this?"

"Love is not self-seeking" (v. 5). While other Scripture says we can expect something out of marriage, love includes this sacrificial attitude. Sex involves a giving of yourself. In the Song of Songs, the woman says to her lover, "Come, and I will give you my love" (based on Song of Songs 7:11–12). Such giving isn't always tiresome. Jesus said it is more blessed (a happy state) to give than receive. And research reveals that the people who enjoy sex the most are the ones who like pleasuring more than they do being pleasured.

"Love is not easily angered" (v. 5). We would understand this better if *anger* were translated "does not fly off the handle." Anger is not always wrong, but love doesn't lose control. If we permit our anger to make us harshly critical or violently abusive, we are obviously not loving. Nor are we if we sulk and harbor bitterness. Adjusting sexually can be upsetting; we'll need to handle our anger with love.

"Love keeps no record of wrongs" (v. 5). Keeping score and getting even is destructive. Peter said that "love covers over a multitude of sins" (1 Pet. 4:8). If you harbor ill feelings and ruminate on them, you can produce enough emotional steam to make you explode like a boiler. How true this is of your lovemaking. Don't take resentments to bed with you.

"Love does not delight in evil but rejoices with the truth" (v. 6). It has been said that you can tell when the honeymoon is over because the couple exchanges saying "You're so wonderful" for "The problem with you is . . ." Faultfinding will wreak havoc with your sex life as nothing else can.

"Love bears all things" (v. 7). Forbearance is the stuff of marriage. Our differences require a certain amount of putting up with each other. A woman had the right idea when she said, "Jack won't pick up his underwear and socks, but he is such a great husband in many other ways that I'll accept the clutter."

"Love always trusts" (v. 7). To doubt someone is not a loving act. But to say "I believe in you" is one of the most supportive things you can do for your partner. Spouses can hold each other accountable for behaving properly around other men and women, but they should be careful not to be overly suspicious.

"Love always hopes" (v. 7). Sometimes one of you will be down, your depression making you see a dark sky in every direction. That's when the other says, "There's hope—things will get better." Apply that same optimism to your lovemaking. Sexual love does have a flavor of hope; theologians have spoken of it. It lies in the act of procreating. Bringing a child into the world expresses some optimism and a futuristic outlook. Pittenger sees an implicit hope in the sexual union because it says, "I will love you forever." In such everlasting love there is hope.[4]

"Love always perseveres" (v. 7). Endurance doesn't mean we accept our marital problems without seeking to solve them. We should try everything, including counseling, to grow together. However, there are times when all we can do is endure. This is love's suffering. Remember that Jesus endured the cross.

"Love never fails" (v. 8). This doesn't mean love always succeeds, as if to say that if we love someone, he or she will love back. It means love will always continue. It lies at the heart of reality, at the very nature of God. "And now these three remain: faith, hope and love. But the greatest of these is love" (v. 13). Marriage will last if love will.

Love Takes Off the Rose-Colored Glasses

Besides being sacrificial, Christlike love is realistic. The sheer magnitude of it is expressed in Paul's statement that "God demonstrates his own love for us in this: While we were still sinners, Christ died for us" (Rom. 5:8). Though he knew who and what we are, he loved us.

Those romantically in love don't always see so clearly. Because it is emotionally based, romantic love is idealistic. Lovers will be blind to each other's problems and faults; each partner is wonderful and beautiful to the other. This idealism may extend to all of life. They live in a fantasy, full of optimism and happiness.[5]

Note how one man's passion radically distorted his perception of reality. "So Jacob served seven years to get Rachel, but they seemed like only a few days to him because of his love for her" (Gen. 29:20). With strong feelings of love, we tend not to see all of the person, or else we dismiss the importance of any faults we do see. We might even distort our own value system for a time. As one man said, "Before we were married, she loved to go sailing with me, and I was thrilled by the evenings at the symphony with her. But after marriage she got sick in the sailboat, and I became nauseated at the symphony." The weakness of romantic love shows up when the illusion fades and reality sets in.

A long-term marriage cannot be sustained on illusion; like Christ's love, it must be realistic. We must eventually love a person for what he or she is, not for what we thought him or her to be. One of the most beautiful statements I have ever read about love is this:

> Acceptance in marriage is the power to love someone and
> receive him in the very moment that we realize how far he or
> she falls short of our hopes. It is love between two people who
> see clearly that they do not measure up to one another's dreams.
> Acceptance is loving the real person to whom one is married.
> Acceptance is giving up the dreams for reality.[6]

This is not to say that marital love is without idealism. Our passion for each other will cause us to overlook each other's faults and even put each other in a favorable light. The other day I mentioned to Ginger that when I look at her I often see the twenty-three-year-old girl I married. She confided that she too sees the youthful me. There's plenty of idealism in that; to see a young man in this gray-haired, bearded, slightly bent, arthritic body is a stretch of the imagination. But love can make that happen, and we were both thrilled to find that Shakespeare wrote of it:

To me, fair friend, you never can be old,
For as you were when first your eye I eyed,
Such seems your beauty still. Three winters cold
Have from the forest shook thee summer's pride,
Three beauteous springs to yellow autumn turned
In process of the seasons have I seen,
Three April perfumes in three hot Junes burn'd,
Since first I saw you fresh, which yet are green.[7]

SHOULD ROMANTIC LOVE SURVIVE IN MARRIAGE?

So far I've suggested that the love Paul urged husbands to have for their wives is committed, sacrificial, and realistic. Now I want to deal with whether love should also be passionate. I used to teach that it shouldn't because I believed that God would not command us to feel an emotion that is outside our control. I taught that God was not asking spouses to feel love but to act in love. They are to love willfully and sacrificially and to show love by their attitude and actions—even if they don't feel like it. I based this on the idea that the term *agape* is different from the Greek word *eros*, which was used to describe the more passionate, emotional side of love.

Even C. S. Lewis thought this, believing it would be unfair of God to ask husbands to "feel love." Lewis argued, "I can't always promise to love you any more than I can promise always to be hungry or never to have a headache." Mary Pride agrees, claiming that "romance is the blossom on the flower of marriage, not the root. It is beautiful, it is a gift of God, but marriage can survive without it." We shouldn't expect it, she says, but we should instead strive for another kind of love. God requires young wives to "'love their husband' (Titus 2:4) and the love He asks from us is *phile* love, brotherly love." It is based on our relationship, not on our emotions.[8] There is a certain truth to that. We must sometimes act as if we love even when we are angry or disappointed.

I agree that a marriage can survive without romance, and it is sometimes appropriate for two people to marry even though they have little romantic feeling beforehand. Lack of feeling toward a spouse is no reason for leaving. Nor does being unloved give grounds for divorce. The basis of marriage is commitment. But commitment to what? Is it merely a pledge to bear children and convey sisterly and brotherly love? Should we expect more, want more, and strive for more? Mary Pride seems to be describing the minimal marriage. But what is an ideal marriage, one toward which we might aspire?

In recent years I have come to believe that we should strive for passion and intensity of feeling in our marriages and that I was wrong to exclude these qualities from Christlike love. The term *agape* does not exclude emotion. Today's biblical scholars do not distinguish *agape* and other types of love as much as they once did. The Greek word *phile* is closely linked to friendship, and the word *eros* is used for erotic feelings. But the words are not always used in such an exclusive way. In the Greek translation of the Old Testament (second century B.C.), the term *agape* is used for sexual intercourse. And *phile* is sometimes used in place of *agape*. So it's clear that *agape* love is not just a willed, unemotional love.

The passage in Ephesians suggests Christ loves us emotionally. The imagery refers to Christ as the bridegroom preparing his bride for the wedding day. The phrase "to make her holy, cleansing her by the washing with water through the word" (Eph. 5:26) refers to the ritual bath the bride would take prior to the wedding. Presenting to himself a "radiant church" pictures the bride on her wedding day, "without stain or wrinkle or any other blemish" (v. 27), no doubt referring to her wedding gown. This passage does not mean that husbands are to do for their wives what Christ does for the church, as if a husband is responsible for making his wife holy. Rather, these specific things Christ does are part of the metaphor that pictures his love. And the picture of that love includes emotion—that of a bridegroom anticipating his marriage to his bride. When Paul asks men to love their wives, he is urging them to feel or at least cultivate a feeling of love, not merely to act as if they love.

Upon hearing this from me, a woman said that it encouraged her because she didn't want her husband just to act as if he loved her, but *really* to love her. After all, when married people ask each other, "Do you love me?" they're asking about feelings, not only actions. It's not fair to say to your spouse, "I will act in love, but don't expect me to feel love for you." We each need to feel loved.

The Old Testament concept of marital love includes emotions, which was another reason to include them in Paul's command to husbands.

Being a Jew, Paul would have thought of Christ and the church in terms of Jewish ideas of the relationship between a bride and a bridegroom, and passion is one element. Numerous Scriptures paint a picture of marriage; the one in the Song of Songs is the most colorful. For centuries Jews have garnished their weddings with its ornate poetry. It sings of love that is deeply personal and intensely emotional. To the bridegroom the woman is darling and beautiful; her "voice is sweet" and her "face is lovely." In her eyes he is handsome and pleasant; her "lover" and her "friend" (Song 2:14; 5:16).

"Love," the Song declares, "is as strong as death, its jealousy unyielding as the grave. It burns like a blazing fire, like a mighty flame. Many waters cannot quench love; rivers cannot wash it away" (Song 8:6–7). It is this sort of love, according to Proverbs, that wives should have for their husbands and husbands should value. "May you rejoice in the wife of your youth. A loving doe, a graceful deer—may her breasts satisfy you always, may you ever be captivated by her love" (Prov. 5:18–19). Christlike love, the kind of love God asks of us in Ephesians, has a tinge of romance in it. One commentator titles this passage "The Romance of Christ and the Church."

Yet this romantic love is somewhat distinct from what is sometimes portrayed in popular culture. Novels and movies picture it as something that happens to us: love between a woman and man is spontaneous, beyond our control. A film entitled *Falling in Love* depicted two people with this frame of mind. On a subway a man's eyes caught those of a woman, starting a love affair between the two married people. As the reels rolled, the couple tumbled into love. All the while the audience is led to cheer for them to leave their drab marriages and stumble helplessly and headlong into the new love. They are compelled to follow love, which summons them like a god. Previous commitments to morality or family are subjected to its power. Nothing else matters.

If we believe our feelings are outside of our control, we can as easily fall out of love as we fell into it. Then we think that we have a basis for separating. A distraught wife persuaded her husband to see me in hopes that I could get him to change his mind. When I asked him why he wanted to leave his wife, he said, "I no longer love her."

Holding this view of love can also cause some anxious moments. "I no longer love my wife; what should I do?" a young man asked me.

Other questions followed quickly, punctuated by the panic that showed on his face. Is it normal for love to vanish? If so, what does that mean? Had he married the wrong girl? Did he really love her in the first place? With feeling gone, could marriage survive? If it did, would he be reduced to sharing a house with a friend, except for periodic romps in the bedroom to relieve lust or conceive children?

To answer these questions, we have to determine whether romantic love is uncontrollable. The Bible sometimes suggests that it is, with Jacob being the most obvious example. This story and the Song of Songs show it is wise for people to be sure they have some feelings of love for the person they are marrying. Feelings of love do arise without effort, but they don't seem to continue without it. Lovers don't automatically live happily ever after.

In some cases love is destroyed by poor handling of conflicts, bad attitudes, and hurtful actions. It doesn't die; it's murdered. In other cases it falls victim to neglect. Too often people fail to make love a priority. I've met men who loved their pickup trucks more than they loved their wives and women who loved their jobs more than their husbands. The Bible also tells us we can and should have some control over our loving. Like a lawn, love needs maintenance. The man who wanted to divorce his wife because he no longer loved her explained that they failed to cultivate their love. Besides both of them having full-time jobs, they bought homes in need of repair, fixing them and selling them for a profit. They spent their lives remodeling houses, with no time to refurbish their marriage.

KEEPING ROMANCE IN YOUR MARRIAGE

The key to keeping love alive is keeping romance in your marriage. Of course, we need to determine what's romantic for us. Though we constantly dream, sing, and talk of falling in love, not all people seem to fall the same way. Two researchers asked forty-eight college students to write down some thoughts about love. After studying the data, they concluded, "Romantic love is not a clear-cut singularly understood phenomenon."[9]

Yet there have been other studies that identify some common elements in people's experience of romance. These components seem to have their origin in our adolescence and early young adult years, when we were ripe for a close encounter with the opposite sex. Certain experiences and feelings that come at that time provide the elements for romantic love.

Admiration. For a young girl, romance means being valued not merely for her body but for herself. It means being cared for, having someone go out of the way to notice her. A woman cannot bask in those teenage fantasies and expectations all her life. But she will probably be disappointed if her husband stops admiring her. If she suffers too much disillusionment, she may escape in romantic novels and daydreams, trying to take flight from a boring relationship.

This is not to say that we can fill every day with wild romance. Daily work will sap our energies. Crises and other problems will distract us. But these are part of the challenge of being romantic in marriage. Anyone can be romantic on a beach in the Bahamas. It will take more effort and creativity to cultivate that same feeling in our backyard or bedroom, especially after the typical struggles at work and hassles with children. We can't always take a cruise across the ocean every year, but we can take an occasional trip to the Captain's Steak Joynt across town.

Intimacy. Part of falling in love includes the thrill of getting to know someone intimately. The hefty football tackle says to his admiring cheerleader girlfriend, "I'm gonna tell you something that I've never told anybody else before." As she gazes into his eyes, her heart beats wildly as this hunk shares a private part of himself with her.

Pampering. Coddling someone is a unique and special way of showing that you are really in love. Andrew Greeley's report of two national Gallup polls on marriage confirmed that people with great marriages were ever spoiling each other. A man once confided that one of the most effective turn-ons for his wife is when he helps her with something she's doing—like peeling potatoes (ever think of spuds as romantic?). Some other suggestions follow.

Him
- Serve her breakfast in bed; put wildflowers on the tray.
- Give her the evening. Do any of her chores for her.

- Draw a bath for her. Add bath oil and float flowers on the water. Light the bathroom with candles and put on music for her. Watch the children, if you have them, and let her soak for as long as she likes.
- Sharpen her kitchen knives.
- Give her a gift certificate for a day at a beauty salon.
- Send her out for the day. Have the house cleaned, or do it yourself.
- Repair something around the house that she has not asked to be done.

Her
- Give him a full body rub.
- Help him on a project.
- If he is out for the evening, greet him when he comes home with a special snack and wear a negligee he particularly likes.
- Borrow his car and have it washed for him.
- Give him a mug full of coupons: "Good for one _____." Include things such as a favorite dessert, a special meal, or a shopping trip for clothes for him.
- If you have children, take them out of the house and give him a night at home alone.
- Send him a package at work, or flowers if he likes them.

Affirmation of gender. Being loved validates us. This is precisely what happens to us during our early romantic episodes. We meet someone who admires us, not just as a person but also as a person of the opposite sex. When people are first in love, they become preoccupied with each other. Because they feel good about each other, they feel good about themselves. After marriage, we still want our partner to want us in this same way. "Say it with flowers," the florists tell us. In our seminars Ginger suggests we "say it with words." However we do it—a word, a surprise gift, a note, a special favor—we keep romance alive by constantly telling our partners what each means to the other: her as a woman to him, him as a man to her. For more on this, see the next chapter.

Sensuality. Romantic love is obviously a sensual experience, but it is not just sexual. Romance precedes sexual contact rather than merely following it. A man's nakedness will probably arouse a woman less than his gentleness will. Both sexes will be aroused by touch, but the first ones need to be soft and in the right context. Being romantic requires us to be sensually suggestive rather than sexually overt. Saying "Let's hop in bed" is not romantic. Sending a box of candy with a note saying, "I can't wait to see you tonight" is. So are other promises of sensual things to come: a room full of candles, a touch on the arm, a flash of leg, a whisper or a wink at a party, a back rub.

Him
- Give her a shampoo; make it a sensual experience.
- Install a colored light in the bedroom.
- Put a recording of ocean waves on the stereo. Play it while you have a nude luau on the living room floor.
- Write her a list of romantic and sensual times you have had together; then discuss them later in the evening.
- Give her a recording of a song that inspires memories of your life together.

Her
- Pour him a bubble bath and get in with him.
- Let him watch you undress.
- Invite him to go skinny-dipping with you.
- If you have children, arrange for them to be gone and then have a romantic, candlelight dinner waiting for him in the evening. Wear something sexy.

Surprise. Romance delightfully surprises us. Falling in love is unpredictable. Adolescents live with the anticipation that it will happen and relish the exhilaration when it does. Meeting and getting to know the person who may become your life partner is an exciting time. Romantics expect some excitement and surprise in their relationship. Generally a wife will not expect marriage to be a trip on the Love Boat, but she does not expect a routine ride on the 7 A.M. commuter train either. Nor do men; most are hopelessly romantic.

Him
- Call her on Tuesday and ask her for a date on Saturday, but don't tell her where you are taking her.

- Buy satin sheets for the bed.
- Bring her a long-stemmed rose for no particular reason.
- Have the menu from her favorite romantic restaurant framed for her.
- Plan a surprise weekend or vacation.
- Bring home a bunch of violets; have her discover them on her pillow.

Her
- Plan a surprise party, decorations and all, for the two of you.
- Arrange to meet him at a hotel for dinner; book a room.
- Initiate lovemaking when he's not expecting it.
- Surprise him with two tickets to a sporting event and take him to it.
- Drop by where he works and take him to lunch.

If some of these ideas seem a bit silly to you, take them for what they are—suggestions to stir your own imagination. But don't reject them too quickly; to your partner they may not be so absurd. A middle-aged man once told me that he had thought a suggestion I made was really dumb. Writing a note to his wife on a mirror telling her what she meant to him was not for him. Yet he confessed that a few days after he heard this idea from me, he printed a message to his wife on the bathroom mirror before he went to work. Then he said, eyes moist, "When I got home from work, my wife said she couldn't wait till I got home to tell me how much that meant to her. I had no idea."

FOR THE LOVE-CHALLENGED

Some of us have a hard time playing the role of lover because our background didn't prepare us well for it. "I really don't know what love is," a twenty-one-year-old man said to me. He was tortured by his inability to fall in love. Though he had been dating girls since high school, he had never felt anything special for any of them. "What's it like to be in love?" he asked. "How will I know when it happens?"

Suspecting a deep personal problem, I asked him to describe his family. "I ran away from home when I was eighteen," he began. "My dad never showed any affection for me." A military man, the father was a harsh disciplinarian, and the mother wasn't affectionate either. This young man left home after his father lost his temper with him because of his hairstyle. "My dad got so mad over my long hair, he began pulling it out by the roots while beating my head against the wall." Hearing her son's screams, his mother stopped his father. The boy quickly fled the house, remembering the pain, the confusion, and the hole in the kitchen plaster his father had used his skull to make. "Do you think I'll ever feel love?" he asked. I offered him hope. But the sting of his past may always to some degree be with him. His experience of love may never be what it might have been.

Childhood experiences make some people obsessed with love. They are anxious lovers who are extremely possessive and often jealous. They cling to their spouses when they are together and dream of them when apart. A compliment or a reassurance lasts for only a few hours. Research reveals that most of these obsessed lovers had a parent or parents who were demanding and distant.

The opposite of the anxious lover is the indifferent or distant partner. Not wanting to be controlled by anyone, he or she will not give in to affection for another. Distant partners hold back something of themselves. Some do it unconsciously, failing to say, "I love you," or writing notes or going out of their way to be a lover. They are unaware that they are giving themselves to their job, a hobby, or other activity. Some hold back deliberately; they have decided not to let affection interfere with their freedom. These indifferent lovers, like the anxious lovers, were the victims of rejection by a parent. They have learned that trying to love deeply can cause deep hurt. They cannot bring themselves to say wholeheartedly what true lovers do: "I am my beloved's, and my beloved is mine." That belongingness reaches a high point in the sexual embrace. We want our lovers to hold back nothing. This can be a problem since some people fear this loss of self. Some women don't have orgasms because they can't let go of themselves. If a person has trouble being owned, he or she may have trouble being interested in sex or in reaching a climax.

There are, of course, other types of dysfunction when it comes to love. But by God's grace, they can be overcome. To free ourselves from the past's hold on us, we must first of all admit our problem, which is usually hard to do. We can easily avoid doing something about our problem by denying we have it. Defensively stating "I have no problem" is only one form of denial. Denial also comes in other guises: minimizing ("I'm not as bad as Jerry"), blaming ("It's her problem; she just wants more love than anyone can give"), or delaying ("I know I should do something, but . . ."). Change in ourselves and our marriage won't happen until we listen to what our partner or others are saying to us and face our shortcoming. It will be encouraging to your partner for you to admit your inability to love as he or she would like and that you will work on doing better.

Once you do that, you can turn it over to God, prayer being your greatest tool of recovery. Ask God for grace for you to face yourself and your problem and see the power of his Spirit.

But these emotional blocks and personality glitches aren't healed or disposed of only by prayer. For this reason the Bible urges us to carry each other's burdens. We must let others into our lives to help us, for the Holy Spirit is available through them. Talking to someone you trust is the most effective way to rid yourself of the dark shadows of the past; a friend, a counselor, or a support group will do. We should be open to our partners but not depend on them alone for support, since it may overburden them.

There are scores of books to guide you in dealing with your past, no matter what it was. We can put the past behind us, not by ignoring it but by facing it. Our backgrounds tint our emotions as dye colors cloth, but the past's pigments are not indelible. They can fade, and our deepest self can undergo change. That is the message of the gospel. God is the greatest lover; he wants us to be lovers too.

❧ *Pillow Talk* ❧

SPEAKING YOUR PARTNER'S LOVE LANGUAGE

People say, "I love you," in different ways. Some do it with a hug, others with a gift. This is called your love language.[10] People also like to be loved in certain ways, normally in the same fashion that they give love. But partners don't love in the ways their spouse wants to be loved because they don't know their partner's love language. Learning it is the purpose of this Pillow Talk.

Step 1: To stimulate your thinking, note these five types of expressions of love:

1. Giving words of affirmation ("I appreciate you.")
2. Serving (doing a chore for your partner)
3. Spending quality time together (taking time to walk with your partner)
4. Giving gifts (a surprise bouquet of flowers)
5. Touching and close contact (a hug at the right time)

Step 2: Each of you (alone) write in the space below five ways your partner expresses love to you that mean the most to you.

_____

_____

_____

_____

_____

Step 3: Each of you (alone) write in the space below five ways you use the most to express love to your partner.

_____

_____

_____

_____

_____

Step 4: One of you begins by comparing your list from step 3 with your partner's list from step 2.

1. Determine if the way you are expressing love is the way your partner most appreciates being loved.
2. Discuss suggestions for improving your love expressions.

Step 5: Now compare your partner's list from step 3 with your list from step 2.

1. Determine if the way your partner is expressing love is the way you most appreciate being loved.
2. Discuss suggestions for improving your partner's love expressions.

Step 6: Evaluate each of your lists to see if there is a pattern to the expressions of love that mean the most to you. Discovering these can help you better express your love in appropriate ways.

Chapter Five

SEX AND PERSONAL IDENTITY

AFFIRMATION MATTERS

*D*uring six years of marriage, Jay had sex with his wife only four times. Describing how his impotence made him feel, he told me, "At the end of the day, toward evening, I get depressed, fearing another disappointing attempt to please my wife. In the morning I have to talk myself into facing another day as a man after failing to be one the night before."

Jay's inadequacy wounded his sense of self because his self-image is tied to his marital sex life, as it is for all of us. This is because God created males and females, thus making our personal identity a matter of gender. To be emotionally healthy we must value ourselves as one or the other. Our erotic desires are fueled in part by a deep need to affirm ourselves. If we are married, our sex life will either boost our self-esteem or, like Jay's, diminish it.

People don't have to be sexually active to have a secure sense of who they are. There are other ways single people can be assured of their femininity and masculinity. Besides, gender is not our most important identity. We are foremost persons created in the image of God, and our most crucial identity is that of being children of God by faith in Jesus Christ. Because Jay was a strong Christian, he was able to maintain his self-respect. But it was a struggle to do so.

IDENTITY'S TWO INGREDIENTS

Two ingredients are involved in self-esteem: knowing who you are and liking who you are. To respect yourself you must first have a clear image of yourself, including your being a man or a woman. Then you will need to value the person you think you are. Acting sexually contributes to both of these aspects. Successfully performing sexually makes us feel good about ourselves as men or women.

A woman who has little or no desire to make love to her husband may face a crisis of personhood. She is not only missing a pleasurable experience but also may feel incomplete as a woman.

Granted, such people can compensate for the missing piece of their identity. Not every married couple must have a sizzling sex life for each of them to feel complete as individuals or as a couple. Sex is only part of the picture, and the crucial issue is whether they experience mutual satisfaction and fulfillment. Just as good marital sex contributes to healthy self-esteem, so healthy self-esteem contributes to good sex. Self-esteem plays a major role in the kind of married partner you will be; the slogan "poor me, poor marriage" is all too true. Low self-esteem will play havoc in the bedroom.

SELF-ESTEEM IN THE BEDROOM

The purpose of this chapter is to link self-regard with sex. As you read it, I hope you'll find ways to boost your self-esteem by improving your sex life as well as improving your sex life by boosting your self-esteem. High self-esteem is important to pleasurable sex in several ways.

Makes Us More Appealing

A woman who is comfortable with herself and her body (no matter what its size or shape) exudes more sex appeal than one who doesn't. Men are turned off by a wife who constantly makes self-deprecating comments about her appearance. Men, too, are more attractive when they accept themselves and appear more confident about who they are, despite any personal and physical limitations.

Makes Us Free to Receive, Able to Give

Self-esteem allows a person the freedom to receive pleasure. Self-regard makes it possible for a person to have fun, to enjoy life. Without it people will feel uncomfortable when others give them a present or a compliment, because they feel unworthy to receive it. This problem is heightened when the gift is sexual pleasure. People with low self-esteem may turn off their erotic feelings because unconsciously they feel they don't deserve them.[1]

Self-regard also enables lovers to give pleasure. Otherwise their uncertainty about themselves makes them feel that they have nothing to offer. A low sense of self can make persons anxious about losing themselves. They fear letting go, which good lovemaking requires, and find it hard to express themselves in bed.

Enables Us to Accept Our Preferences

Self-esteem also allows persons to admit and accept their own tastes and pleasures, which is important because pleasures vary a lot from individual to individual. Part of successful lovemaking is doing what we want to do, not what others think we should do. Without some measure of self-esteem, lovers won't feel free to pursue their desires. Not valuing themselves, they won't ask their partner for what they would like. They may fear their partners will reject them or do something that makes them feel uncomfortable about who they are. In fact, some therapists claim that such people may actively discourage their partners from stimulating them effectively.[2] People with self-regard also feel the freedom to search for novel ways to gratify themselves and their sexual partners, keeping the relationship fresh.

Gives Us Faith to Overcome

Being sure of yourself will also help you to overcome sexual problems. Signs of dissatisfaction or disinterest in sex by either partner on a honeymoon can devastate a person who is uncertain of himself or herself. The more secure a person's identity, the less there will be fear of failure or rejection. We have to accept our own sexuality, or else we become our own worst problem—and our partner's.

Allows Others to Be Themselves

Finally, persons who accept and value themselves will also tend to accept and value their partners, giving them the freedom to be themselves. Developmental psychologist Erik Erikson has shown how we need to have a valid sense of self before we can be truly intimate. We must be at least in our early twenties for this to happen, he claims. Before this, we haven't established a personal identity. True intimacy requires accepting people as they are, something adolescents seem to be incapable of doing. Because they are in the process of finding themselves, adolescents are self-absorbed. They build relationships because they see the other person as an extension of some characteristic of their own. A boy hangs out with jocks because he thinks of himself as one. Other athletes confirm his identity, which is still in the formative stage. The other person is an object or instrument for enhancing his view of himself. After identity is more intact, it is possible for a person to form a mature, close relationship. A jock will see no threat in having an actress or a scholar as a close friend.

An unformed identity may be expressed in one of several self-centered ways. A woman loves her husband because he thinks she is someone special. ("He adores my body.") A husband loves his wife because she gives him prestige or status. ("I look good with her on my arm.") Or each loves the other because they go with each other's idealized ego. ("Her being a professor affirms my own intelligence.") The results of immature love can be gruesome. An abusive and domineering husband is a terrible example of an underdeveloped self. He can't stand his wife being a woman on her own terms; rather, she must conform to his ideal, or she is a threat to him. A mature lover will allow his wife to be different, loving her for what she is, not what he expects her to be.

People with a lack of self-regard may also depend too much on their partners for personal validation. Men especially are prone to do this. They make their sense of manhood dependent on their wife's sexual responses, watching constantly for them. Her moans and screams signal his male virility, which in turn confirms his identity. When she interprets his need for her reactions as a demand, it puts enormous pressure on her. This makes it more difficult for her to respond because passions don't respond well to being pressured. They are a bit like cats: Do what you can to make them come to you, but you can't be sure they will. Responding to her husband as he wants will become especially difficult for a wife when his demands are excessive. And the demands will be excessive if a man has an oversized need to prove his manhood in bed. The same will be true of a woman who has a similar need for validation. She may constantly insist on her husband's sexual attention and performance, feeling cheated if he doesn't give her enough orgasms or otherwise fulfill her expectations.

Men and women who need such personal validation will have to work hard at relieving the stress this places on their spouses. First, they need to recognize that it places both them and their spouses in an impossible situation. No man or woman, regardless of sexual prowess, can make a sexual partner respond all the time. Because men are so achievement oriented, they are prone to overload their wives sensually. What counts on their scoreboard is quantity, not quality. To fill the void, they demand more of a wife than she can give. This ends up reducing her passion, making the problem worse. Clifford and Joyce Penner advise men to keep their sexual activity just a bit less than a wife would want. This keeps her hungry without starving her and helps her maintain her desire for him.[3]

People who use sex to prove themselves must also learn to be satisfied with the response they get from their partners and stop watching for their reactions. They should instead focus on their own pleasure. This will help relieve the pressure on the spouse, enabling him or her to respond more spontaneously. Most of all they need to work on other ways to maintain their sense of identity and then bring a more secure self into the bedroom instead of trying to establish it there.

GAINING AND MAINTAINING SELF-ESTEEM

For the sake of yourself and your partner, you need to value yourself. The fact that many of us have trouble doing this is apparent from the many books about self-esteem that are published. Whether or not self-esteem is a serious problem for you, there are things you can do to gain and maintain your self-respect.

Discard False Shame

Start by dealing with any unresolved issues of your childhood. Past family life is no doubt behind an excessive need to prove oneself through sex. A case in point is the woman who constantly wanted men to pursue her aggressively, even though she remained passive. Their unsolicited attention made her feel attractive, something she badly wanted. Rivalry with her sister created this need in her. When she was growing up, she was painfully aware that her pretty sister got attention from boys that she didn't. Now she fills her exorbitant need to feel feminine and attractive through sex.[4]

Many types of family experiences can make people feel badly about themselves. A student from an abusive, alcoholic family told me, "Whenever I go to a social event, I feel like I don't belong, that somehow I am different. All evening long I fight the feeling that someone is going to come up to me and say, 'Please leave; you don't belong here.'" For him life is a party to which he wasn't invited. His parents failed to welcome him into the world, which is one of their jobs. When through neglect, ridicule, or physical abuse, they don't, a child may feel isolated and unwanted.

Psychologists dub this attitude "shame," which is not the same as embarrassment. Persons with this type of shame are not merely embarrassed by their actions; they are ashamed of their existence. It helps to know how a family, perhaps yours, produces people who are so down on themselves. Sometimes it's a lack of affirmation. Perhaps a child never heard, "You handled that well," or, "You are talented." Instead the child may have heard, "You should be ashamed of yourself," or, "You'll never amount to anything, stupid."

Perhaps lack of self-esteem may grow out of perfectionism, a trait common to people reared in dysfunctional families. Because the situation is often harsh, a child will fantasize about a better life. If dad called his daughter a slut when he was drunk or while he was assaulting her, she imagined herself to be a princess. Such imaginings cause children to form images of themselves and life that they can't possibly fulfill.

The simplest explanation of shame and lack of self-regard may be the intensity of the disgraceful things that happened to someone. I've heard people in support groups talk about seeing someone carry a drunken father up the porch steps, hearing their parents shout at each other in public, or looking out the window at the flashing lights of a police car in the driveway.

Neglect too can contribute to lack of self-love. Parents care for, protect, and encourage us. When they do, we then value ourselves. However, if parents don't do these things, we feel undervalued. I once tried to help an overweight woman understand the basis of her lack of self-esteem. She admitted she didn't like herself and didn't see how she could be attractive. "When did you last feel pretty?" I asked her. "Once, when I got a special dress for a father-daughter banquet at our church. This was just a few weeks after my dad left our home and filed for divorce. After getting the dress, I called to invite him to go with me, but he said he was too busy." At a crucial time in her development, when she needed her father's validation, she got only his rejection.

Lack of a father's affirmation can often cause a woman to be troubled in one of two ways. She may become promiscuous, jumping into bed with man after man in an effort to confirm her femininity. Or she may be clumsy and shy in her relationships with men. Either of these disabilities can follow a woman into marriage.

A boy without a father may have one of two problems. He may be an insensitive macho type, acting out his stereotype of a man. Because he didn't have a male role model who could have shown him the softer side of a man, he acts out the only image he knows. If he doesn't become insensitive, he may be homosexual. Although not all gay men have this background, some do.

Dysfunctional families are not merely those that were abusive or addictive. Any sort of troubled person can create a dysfunctional family: a workaholic, a gambler, an angry person, or someone who is religiously compulsive.

This leads to neglect of other family members' needs. They are so dominated by someone else's life that they have little life of their own. Not only might they have little self-respect, they may have little sense of self to respect. They may be confused about who they are and be shy about standing up for themselves. A man describes his experience: "Suppose someone has just had a bad day and is tense. If that person was short with me or made a bad remark to me, even if it was not the truth, I would assume I was wrong, even though I wasn't." For some people the sense of self is so small that they can't distinguish what they feel from what others feel. Thus they don't even know what they are feeling because their feelings don't matter.

Any review of your self-esteem and your attitude toward sex requires some scrutiny of your past. It's worthwhile to take a good look at it, and if you do discover some negative impact on your personal identity, deal with it. (At the end of this book, I've included a list of books that will help you to look at your past.) Besides inspecting your family tree, there are other things you can do.

Realize Love Isn't Just for Others

We must build proper self-esteem by realizing that it is OK to love ourselves. Research has shown that such love is an indication of mental health. Yet some Christians dispute this, claiming that Scripture commends self-sacrifice, not self-love. Self takes second place to others, they insist, quoting the apostle Paul: "In humility consider others better than yourselves" (Phil. 2:3).

Christians are to live unselfishly, but that doesn't exclude loving themselves. This principle is implied in the command to love your neighbor as yourself. We are to love others because they are of worth, just as we are. When Paul tells us to consider others better than ourselves, he doesn't ask us to deny our own needs. He says, "Each of you should look not only to your own interests, but also to the interests of others" (Phil. 2:4). Our needs are important too. The worth of every human being is a cardinal doctrine of Christian faith, a doctrine that is based on the fact that every person is created in the image of God. For this reason murder is terrible (Gen. 9:6), and cursing others is wrong (James 3:9–10). Why then should we diminish ourselves?

Own Your Self-Image

Like many of us, Margaret was convinced that until she could get her father to love her she would never feel good about herself. But whenever people place the standard of approval outside themselves, they are in trouble. Setting an external standard requires you to win that approval. When approval depends on someone else, you are trapped into thinking, "I am not what I think I am; I am not what you think I am; I am what I think you think I am."

To spring from this trap, you must seize ownership of your self-image. You decide to be the one who sets the standards of self-approval. I'll grant that God has his standards for us, and we'll discuss those in a moment. But his ideals for us are not always embodied in ideals other people have set for us. The apostle Paul wrote, "I care very little if I am judged by you or by any human court; indeed, I do not even judge myself. My conscience is clear, but that does not make me innocent. It is the Lord who judges me" (1 Cor. 4:3–4). We must avoid marching to other people's drumbeat, or we'll never know the joy of dancing to our own and God's tune.

Base Self-Esteem on Forgiveness

When we are dealing with how we feel about ourselves, we must take into account that we are sinners. There are times when we ought to feel ashamed and guilty. But feeling bad that we've sinned is not the same as feeling bad that we are alive. Nothing should rob us of our sense of worth, not even our most terrible offenses, failures, or faults. Note that Adam and Eve's fall into sin did not destroy the fact that people are still created in the image of God (Gen. 9:6; James 3:9).

Besides being in God's image, we as Christians have a new identity in Christ. In him we are new creatures who "have put on the new self, which is being renewed in knowledge in the image of its Creator" (Col. 3:10). The New Testament describes vividly the traits of the new self as love, joy, peace, patience, kindness, goodness, faithfulness, gentleness, self-control, and compassion, along with other traits like Jesus'. The Bible tells us to put on these things and also to picture them as already "put on" (Col. 3:10). Even though we fall short of this picture, we are to maintain it in our minds. Because of our faith in Christ, we have been elevated to a new position. In this position we are to consider ourselves accepted by God, forgiven, and part of his family. Otherwise we'll be obsessively involved in endless activity to prove ourselves.

Stop Trying to Prove Yourself

In the early years of my ministry, I sought to do this, not realizing what a poor self-image I had. Speaking to a group of college students at a camp, I said, "Be honest with others, because you have nothing to lose since you are nothing to begin with." I then quoted Paul: "'Neither he who plants nor he who waters is anything, but only God' (1 Cor. 3:7). We were just a piece of junk before Christ saved us."

After my speech, a Christian psychologist who had been in the audience came to me, peered down at me, and angrily said, "Never again tell these people that they are nothing." Then he quoted Francis Schaeffer: "Man is sinful, but he is not junk." I was dumbstruck. What could I say? He was right. I slipped back to my cabin as quickly as I could to keep many people from seeing the red in my face and to set my thinking straight. Worth isn't found in accomplishments, I thought, or in Christ's saving us, but in something even more basic: We are created by God. Christ came to save us because we were of worth to begin with. Then I said to myself, "I have worth sitting here doing nothing."

Never before had I felt so relaxed. My attitude toward myself had changed drastically. My battle with self-esteem wasn't over, but it was at a new stage. I felt a new inner strength and peace. Prior to this I was like a house built on the wrong foundation. Now I have a solid foundation that neither the winds of failure nor storms of sin can move. No matter how much I fail or how little I accomplish, I have worth.

Say Good-bye to Perfectionism

I still had another problem to deal with, and that was perfectionism. We have to face perfectionism for what it is—pride. When we set our standards higher than we can achieve, we are doing what Paul urged us not to do: "Do not think of yourself more highly than you ought" (Rom. 12:3). Perfectionists try to prove themselves by being better than they are. We want to be flattered, and the result is that our low self-esteem stems from thinking too highly of ourselves. To attack this mentally unhealthy virus, we need a good dose of humility. "Think of yourself with sober judgment, in accordance with the measure of faith God has given you," Paul said (Rom. 12:3).

True humility is not negating ourselves but measuring ourselves realistically. We must amputate from our conscience our unrealistic goals and standards.

Brainwash Yourself

To gain more self-acceptance, you must do a bit of brainwashing. Negative images are lodged securely inside our skulls and have to be crowded out by positive ones. When you face a challenge, say, "I can do it," instead of, "I'll never make it." When you tackle personal problems, tell yourself, "By God's grace, I'll eventually overcome," instead of, "I'll be this way forever." When you look at one of your negative traits, replace "I am so compulsive" with "By the Holy Spirit's power, I am self-disciplined."

A positive attitude is not wishful thinking; it's getting your mind off the can'ts and onto the cans, moving from thinking "me, the failure" to "me, the victor."

Let Others Help You

Self-esteem is not something we can trump up only by ourselves. Since we are social creatures, self-esteem grows out of being accepted and affirmed by others. A group in which we feel we belong gives us a warm sense of being worthwhile. It helps, if possible, to be reconciled with our parents if we have been alienated from them. We should try to keep in touch with relatives and others to whom we ought to be close. Drawing on others for support is crucial, especially for those who have been badly hurt in their childhood families. We all need friends as a fan club to love us as we are, and our spouse should be its president.

BE YOUR PARTNER'S MOST LOYAL FAN

You can be your partner's most important cheerleader. Married people are in the best position to boost a partner's self-esteem and confirm his or her identity as male or female. Note how the lovers of the Song of Songs praise each other's sensuality: "How beautiful you are, my darling! Oh, how beautiful!" the man says (Song 4:1). Then he proceeds to describe her feminine charms, beginning with her eyes and moving downward to her breasts. At another time his eyes wander from her feet to her head. The picturesque phrases leave no doubt he sees her as a woman: "Your graceful legs are like jewels. . . . Your breasts are like two fawns. . . . Your neck is like an ivory tower. . . . Your hair is like royal tapestry" (Song 7:1, 3–5). The woman says what every man would love to hear from his wife. She describes his body as "polished ivory," his arms as "rods of gold," his legs as "pillars of marble." "His mouth is sweetness itself; he is altogether lovely" (Song 5:14–16).

A great sex life—and marriage—thrives on affirmation. John Gottman and his colleagues found that in a satisfying, long-term marriage, partners were nice to each other five times for every one time they were nasty.[5] It didn't matter whether they fought a lot or not; what mattered was this ratio of five positives to one negative. Couples can handle conflict and feel good about each other if they continually validate each other. Affirmation can be done in many ways: touching, smiling, complimenting. Birthday and wedding anniversary cards along with a personal note are among the obvious. Then there are more creative affirmations:

Her
- Leave a Post-it note on the car dashboard telling him of one of his qualities you appreciate.
- Say positive things about him in the presence of your children and other people.
- Talk with him about his hobby or special interest.
- Invite him out for coffee and ask him questions about himself.
- Enclose encouragement cards or love notes in his lunch.
- Make a tape recording of all the reasons you have for loving him.

Him
- Send her a telegram telling what you like about her.
- Leave a message on the answering machine praising her.
- Tell her mother what a great woman she is (her mother will tell her).
- Make a list of all the things you like about her; then share one with her each day for the next twenty or thirty days.
- Use the phrase "That's a great idea" a lot.
- Notice what she does around the house and thank her.
- Listen to her talk about her dreams or favorite activities.
- When you pray together, thank God for her.

While you are concentrating on complimenting each other, try limiting the negative comments. We especially have to avoid saying and doing things that demean our partner's gender. Bad jokes and sarcastic comments not only will hurt your partner but also will wreak havoc on your sex life. I have often told men, "If you put your wife down in the living room, it will be harder to put her down in the bedroom." Of course, I'd give the same advice to wives.

Gender image is a real problem for people, especially for women. Husbands badly need to help their wives feel good about their bodies since our culture so ferociously urges upon them a stereotype of feminine beauty portrayed by fashion models. These youthful, willowy figures portray an ideal that is beyond most women, as well as beyond reason. Yet, according to Dr. Andrew Feldman, director of sports medicine at St. Vincent's Hospital in New York, many women go to untenable means to achieve this ideal. He says some of his patients work out three hours a day, seven days a week, or regularly run twenty miles at a time and end up with repetitive stress injuries.[6]

Unbelievable numbers of people risk their health as well as their lives when they try hazardous diets or plastic surgery so they can fit this idea of attractiveness. Some diets put such strain on the kidneys, liver, and heart that the dieters may not be around to enjoy the results of the diet. The same is true for plastic surgery. Liposuction, currently the most popular cosmetic surgical procedure in America, is more likely to kill you than is a traffic accident.[7] People are also taking diet pills that have been proved lethal and exercising until they break bones.

The goal of this pursuit is youth and a certain type of beauty that we are told men are attracted to, and women fear their husbands will chase after younger women. Some evolutionists say men are programmed to like women who show signs of youth and supple beauty, to symmetry, to the waist-to-hip ratio at which women are most likely to conceive and bear babies.[8]

But other researchers claim that this stereotype of attractiveness is cultural, created by the media. Susan Bordo, a professor at the University of Kentucky, studies the impact of media on self-esteem. She claims that the images of fashion models with perfect, airbrushed bodies and pencil-thin actresses have become so pervasive that we've lost a sense of our physical limits. "Advertising, entertainment, medicine, technology, each in its own way, is telling us we don't have to get old," she says.[9]

That this concept of beauty is an invention of modern pop culture is obvious. Else we'd be forced to conclude that the great Renaissance artists had no eye for beauty and sensuality when they embodied it in women who by today's standards would be unpleasantly plump. Perhaps, too, they saw the loveliness of the soul as well as the body, even in the nudes they painted.

Both men and women must confront unrealistic cultural ideas of attractiveness. Though women need to exercise and dress to look their best, they have to resist being dissatisfied with their bodies and avoid unnecessary, risky means to change them. Confronting the media hype, we men need to maintain a sensible concept of beauty and not make our wives feel they are being unfavorably compared with other women. We need to realize that body type or shape has little to do with being a good sex partner. Then we need deliberately and constantly to tell our wives what their bodies mean to us, repeatedly calling attention to their feminine charms. I have had women tell me that their husbands would not tell them they loved them until they lost a certain amount of weight. This is as unwise as it is unkind, creating pressure that will more likely cause a woman to gain pounds by using food to ease the pain of such criticism.

Wives can help their husbands admire them by displaying for their husbands what they have to offer. Women have told us that they are so ashamed of their bodies that they don't like to let their husbands see them. Instead, wives should try to dress or undress in a way that pleases their partners. When my wife, Ginger, speaks on this subject, she encourages all women, especially middle-aged and older women, not to hesitate to reveal their charms. "Not all of us can be a 10 [have the perfect figure]," she says, "and age takes its physical toll. But, after all, your body is the one he has grown to love. Although it's familiar, it is a reminder to him of the countless past pleasures it has given him. The stretch marks and bulges may be reminders of the children the two of you have conceived in love. Remember, it is his body too."

In our youth-oriented culture the need for this affirmation increases as we grow older, since most of us have some anxiety about aging. Ginger displayed some of this concern once when she said to me, "Oh, I'm going to be fifty soon." Sensing her mood—something I haven't always done well—I replied, "I can hardly wait; I've never made love to a fifty-year-old woman before."

BE POSITIVELY NEGATIVE

Because in marriage it's so easy to trample on each other's self-esteem, we should take care in how we criticize each other. When Gottman says that the ratio of negative interaction to positive interaction should be one to five, he claims being nasty is just as important as being nice. In other words, criticism is healthy; we need to tell our spouse when something is troubling us. Otherwise our displeasure will simmer and eventually boil over in hurtful ways. Besides, we can't improve our marriage unless we talk about what needs to be fixed.

But in a good marriage it's crucial to share your negative feelings in a positive way. Timing is important. A critical remark when you're making love can change the mood as quickly as a click of the remote changes a channel. Choose another time to say, "You're not trying hard enough," or, "Why don't you try something different?"

When you do criticize, do it in the most positive way possible. Making a hypothetical statement can take the edge off a bit: "It seems that you don't try hard enough." Or share your displeasure as a feeling instead of a judgment: "You don't ever want to try anything different" becomes "I feel disappointed that we don't try new things." That way our partners are less likely to feel accused. And if they are sensitive to our feelings, they may be more willing to deal with the issue.

Saying no to each other's sexual advances should also be done carefully since such rejection cuts to the core of our sexual identity. We should give each other the freedom to ask for whatever he or she desires, but we should also grant each other the right to refuse. Then we should decline as graciously as we can, making sure being refused does not feel like being rejected. Take time to explain why, and try not to make excuses. We can affirm even when refusing: "I just can't get with it tonight, but I know I won't be able to stay away from a man like you for long" eases a husband down gently.

Affirm each other by sharing what your sexual encounters mean to you. Be specific. Tell each other what you like about your partner and his or her lovemaking. Men want to know that their wives are enjoying what is happening between them. But most of all we need to point out the inner beauty we see in our spouses. Like God, we need to look not on the outward appearance but on the inner person. Realizing we all can't have the most attractive bodies, we can encourage each other to be beautiful persons. It is the masculinity and femininity under the skin that marriage should nurture.

KNOW THY BODY

Besides certifying your spouse's femininity or masculinity, you need to affirm your own. This includes accepting and understanding your body and its functions. Feeling good about yourself as a man or a woman includes accepting your physical apparatus. Any level of disgust with any part of yourself can interfere with your sex life or at least prevent you from developing and enriching it. A woman, for example, who thinks disgustingly of her vulva as "down there" may be shocked and repulsed by her husband's interest in caressing and kissing it.

Physicians and sex therapists report that many people, especially women, dislike or are indifferent to their genitals. It's amazing that some people can be enthralled by a sunset but not awed by how God has wonderfully made them. Treatment of people with sexual disorders includes urging them to become familiar with themselves through self-examination. Charts, pictures, and diagrams in sex manuals can aid both men and women to use their hands and fingers to explore without embarrassment the parts of their reproductive system and to become acquainted with their names and functions. A woman should use a mirror as she explores her vulva's outer and inner lips; her clitoris, hood, and shaft; as well as the interior of the vagina. When they are exploring, both men and women should discover areas of sensitivity. Chapter 6 will describe these so-called erogenous zones and their role in enhancing your lovemaking.

If you're unwilling or unable to make this self-examination, I would advise you to consider seeing a counselor, for obtaining this self-knowledge is critical to being a good sex partner as well as feeling right about who you are.

ASSERT YOUR IDENTITY

When a man says to his wife, "You make me feel like a man," he is referring not only to what she does but also to who she is. Since she is the opposite sex, interacting with her sexually and otherwise makes him feel opposite. Thus the more feminine she is, the more masculine he feels.

Therefore we will affirm our partner's sexual identity by asserting our own. The key to doing this is knowing what your partner's idea of the opposite sex is. Since there are many different ideas about what is masculine and feminine, we need to be sure we are expressing ourselves in our partner's terms, not ours. A husband who tries to be a macho type the guys in the locker room admire may not get a good response from his wife. She may not want a strong, silent man but one who is open and gentle as well as strong. A wife too may fail to understand what her husband wants in a woman.

It's not always easy to know what each of you wants in a partner because views of male and female roles are always changing. The best way is to ask, and some things are rather easy to talk about. A husband can ask if his wife wants him to open the car door for her, and she can ask if he wants her to wear lacy negligees. But it may be difficult to find out about some of our partner's preferences, since those preferences might pose a threat if a partner is unable or unwilling to meet them. A wife may want her husband to share his feelings with her more than he does, but he may think that doing so isn't manly, or he may find it hard to do. A husband may want his wife to talk more about sex, but she may feel inhibited or that it is unwomanly. We should be careful not to excessively demand what we want when our partner is unable to deliver. And we must be patient; it takes time for us to learn to express our masculinity and femininity in terms of our mates. But as we grow old together and make the effort, it can happen.

Marriage is one of the mirrors we look at to discover and maintain who we are. When we are in love, we see ourselves through our lover's eyes. It's hard to be positive about yourself if the one you care about is negative. Abused wives will tell you how tough that is. The barrage of angry condemnation brutally erodes their self-esteem until it shows in the downcast expression of their weary, worn faces.

Yet the affirmation of a loving spouse is as powerful or more so than the condemnation of an abusive one. And this too can be seen on faces. Charlie Shedd, once a popular speaker on family matters, said that whenever he met a radiant elderly woman, one who exuded confidence and serenity, he would try to meet her husband. He suspected that he would find a warm, pleasant, positive man who through a lifetime of affirmation had helped make his wife to be the woman she was. And he usually did. Enough said. Go find your lover and tell him or her how special he or she is to you.

❧ *Pillow Talk* ❧

IDENTIFYING IDENTITY ISSUES

Use the following items as a guide to your talking about your personal identity as well as learning how you can better help each other improve your self-esteem.

Increasing Self-Esteem

Which of the following do you most need to do to gain and maintain your self-esteem?

- Discard false shame.
- Realize love isn't just for others.
- Own your self-image.
- Base self-esteem on forgiveness.
- Stop trying to prove yourself.
- Say good-bye to perfectionism.
- Brainwash yourself into believing you can.
- Let others help you.

Affirming Each Other

Each of you share with your partner what he or she does or says that affirms you (such as verbal compliments, love notes, honoring your mate's suggestions, listening).

Discuss how you can improve your affirmation of one another.

Asserting Your Masculinity or Femininity

For wives: Share with your husband how he asserts his masculinity in ways that make you feel like a woman.

For husbands: Share with your wife how she asserts her femininity in ways that make you feel like a man.

Discuss how you can improve your expressions of masculinity and femininity to enhance each other and your relationship.

Chapter Six

SEX AND PLEASURE

DRINK DEEP OF LOVE

*D*rink your fill, O lovers." With this poetic line, a chorus of young women in the Song of Songs urges the book's main characters to gorge themselves with love (Song 5:1). Such an invitation might seem out of place in the Bible. We might expect instead to see it on a glossy magazine cover at a store checkout counter. Such titles can easily rile our Christian sensibilities: "Savage Love," "101 Great Quickies," "Fun Sex," "Hot Sex," "203 Ways to Drive a Man Wild in Bed," and on and on. If the titles don't irk us, then the promiscuity the articles recommend will. "I thought my lust life with my beau couldn't get any better than our all-night mattress sessions," says Lisa, a twenty-five-year-old market researcher. "Then last weekend, we had a tawdry tryst in a friend's bathroom. I never knew five minutes could be so earth-shattering."[1]

LOVE'S OK, BUT LUST?

Besides the sanction of nonmarital sex, the romping in raw, down-and-dirty sex is bound to make us ask if we can really approve of relishing sex for pure erotic pleasure. Lust can sometimes be such a destructive force. It's behind teenage pregnancies, sexual abuse, various sexually transmitted diseases, and all sorts of crimes and disasters. Because of this, a woman in one of my marriage seminars questioned, "Wouldn't we be better off without sex?"

From the counseling Ginger and I have done, we've learned that many Christians would answer yes to that question. They can't seem to cast lust in a positive light. They merely tolerate lovemaking, seemingly unable to believe they can be sexy and spiritual at the same time. One man's complaint reveals a typical attitude: "My wife flits from one Bible study to another, looking so devout, yet she leaves me sexually starved. Sure, I want a godly wife, but I want a lusty one too. Why can't she be both?"

Some passages of Scripture might suggest that she can't. Peter denounces the "sinful desires, which war against your soul" (1 Pet. 2:11). John censures "the lust of the eyes" and "the lust of the flesh." These are not of the Father, he warns, but are of the world (1 John 2:16–17). And Paul counsels us to walk in the Spirit so that we will not "gratify the desires of the sinful nature" (Gal. 5:16). Such cautions cause some Christians to reject eroticism as a legitimate diversion. Mary Pride advises Christian women not to expect such pleasures: "To do so insists that kicks and thrills are the reasons for marriage and that it turns us into hedonistic adolescents."[2]

As we have seen, there have been Christian thinkers who agree with her, including the formidable Augustine, who contended that to have sex for pleasure was to consent to the depravity of the fallen nature. Even in marriage, sex always included "an element of evil."[3] When having sex to conceive children, he advised, couples should avoid the lust and pleasure that go with it. Because they were influenced by Greek philosophy, these theologians harbored a dismal view of passion. They had learned from Plato and other philosophers that spirit and matter are hostile to each other, spirit being good, matter evil.

Christians who adopted this idea believed that anything physical is an enemy of the soul. The aim of every true Christian, they taught, is to attain perfection through renunciation of the world and subjugation of the body. To this end every means was employed—fasting, solitude, prayer, mortification—but always, as one historian notes, "The decisive test, the critical discipline, was that of sexual continence."[4] An old English marriage service stated that marriage does not exist "to satisfy men's carnal lusts and appetites, like brute beasts that have no understanding."[5]

This view seems to linger in the minds and consciousness of some people perhaps because it was passed down by parents and grandparents who were exposed to it. As recently as 1939, a Roman Catholic marriage manual supported the idea that married couples who abstained from sex had a higher form of marriage. It advised them to abstain from sex for long periods of time because doing so was of "moral worth."[6]

About one hundred years ago, in the Victorian Age, an extremely dim view of marital sex infected America's minds.[7]

Prominent physicians warned of the health hazards of sex, which in their eyes was both sinful and pathological. In this view almost all evil and health problems were related to the nervous shock of orgasm, which had symptoms much like those of epilepsy. Masturbation was the cause of insanity and crime.[8] They counseled married couples to have "calm sex." Sexual intercourse should occur "very seldom" and should be of moderate intensity.[9] Both clergy and physicians urged couples not to have sex often.

Giving in to one's passions could lead to all sorts of maladies ranging from tuberculosis to insanity to cancer of the womb, and it also led to more intense depravity for the race.[10]

Graham advised married people to limit their sexual encounters to once a month. Thirty years later, in 1869, twin beds became popular for married couples who wanted to avoid contact that would arouse them.

Diet was also considered important in curbing sexual passion. Believing that spicy foods excited sexual passion, Dr. John Kellogg invented cornflakes as a cure for sexual arousal. For the same reason Graham invented graham crackers, which were made of unbolted flour. Sex, these people thought, was a disease in need of medical and dietary treatment. These views had a profound influence on how people thought about marriage and family. If a husband and wife were to enjoy romantic and physical intimacy, a wife would have to fight thinking of herself as a prostitute and her husband battle feeling like a corrupt sinner.[11]

Contemporary medical opinion is starkly different. In *Passionate Sex,* Daniel Stein demonstrates how sex contributes to sustaining sound health, preserving youthful spirit, and amplifying a sense of well-being.[12] Sex, he claims, is not just a tonic for tired relationships; *"it is medicine in its most holistic, broadest terms"* (italics his).[13]

LUST IS OK AFTER ALL

Bible scholars and theologians now agree lust is OK; sexual pleasure is no longer censured. The Greek word for "lust" in the New Testament really means "appetite," and the appetites the Bible denounces are evil, fleshly, and youthful ones. Bodily appetites are not on the list. The phrase "fleshly lusts" does not refer to these, since the phrase is a metaphor for the sinful nature. Such sinful lusts should not be confused with legitimate appetites. It's OK for a wife to lust for her husband but not for the man next door, just as it is OK for her husband to desire strongly his wife's body but not that of another woman.

The Bible says a lot of negative things about our carnal cravings because they are extremely powerful and can lead to perverse and destructive acts. But the Bible also has many positive things to say about the pleasures of sex. That the Scripture prods the lovers of the Song of Songs to drink their fill makes clear that God intended sex to be a delicious experience. Taken as a celebration of marital love, this Old Testament song vividly portrays love's delicacies. Of his lover, the man says, "How beautiful you are and how pleasing, O love, with your delights! Your stature is like that of the palm, and your breasts like clusters of fruit" (Song 7:6–7). The woman is unashamedly aware of her feminine charms. Comparing herself with a garden, she invites, "Let my lover come into his garden and taste its choice fruits" (Song 4:16). Scripture often mixes images of drinking with sensuality. "Your love is more delightful than wine" (Song 1:2). "I have come into my garden, my sister, my bride; . . . I have drunk my wine and my milk. Eat, O friends, and drink; drink your fill, O lovers" (Song 5:1).

In the Book of Proverbs, a man is urged to rejoice in the wife of his youth. "A loving doe, a graceful deer—may her breasts satisfy you always, may you ever be captivated by her love" (Prov. 5:19). In addition to the reference to her breasts, there is no doubt that the passage refers to sensuality since the word for "love" is used primarily of the special relationship between married people. The command to be captivated exudes passion; elsewhere the word is used to describe someone who is drunk. A husband is told to be intoxicated by his wife's eroticism. This positive stance toward sex remains in the New Testament. God has given us all good things to enjoy, said Paul, marriage among them. He claims that false prophets who teach doctrines of demons teach otherwise. These false prophets forbid marriage and command to abstain from meat, yet both gifts are "to be received with thanksgiving" (1 Tim. 4:3).

Our physical bodies testify to their capacity for sensual enjoyment, and there is no reason to think this was not part of God's original creation. A woman's clitoris, for example, exists solely for her pleasure, playing no part in conception. Its existence, along with other erogenous zones of both men and women, strongly suggests their Creator wants us to enjoy sensual pleasure.

Besides, lovemaking is free. It's an affront to materialism, which insists we must buy, use, or own something to have fun. For the joy of sex, we need nothing—not even clothes. We need only each other—and God—for these enchanting moments. And having him there makes it even more remarkable because we know our passion for each other is fueled by his love for us.

And lovemaking is a great form of recreation, at times like a short vacation. Lovers, after being lost in each other, after having shut out the world, return to their familiar environment refreshed and renewed. Passion is also a powerful bond. Any shared experience binds people together, whether it is praying or playing. Think of what effect years of shared erotic moments can have on a couple's relationship. It is not only acceptable but also advisable for couples to master the art of making love.

ARTFUL LOVERS

Keep It High on the List

Artful loving starts with giving your sex life proper priority. One of the most sensual sentences ever written is in the Bible: "Let's drink deep of love till morning; let's enjoy ourselves with love!" (Prov. 7:18). This sentence flows from the lips of an unfaithful wife, dressed as a prostitute, trying to entice a stranger into her bed for the night. Why wouldn't the same invitation be appropriate for a wife to give to her husband? Note how meticulously the woman has prepared her seduction: "I have covered my bed with colored linens from Egypt. I have perfumed my bed with myrrh, aloes and cinnamon" (Prov. 7:16–17). The same sort of allurement will enrich any couple's love life. Yet it will take some time and effort.

This is especially true during certain seasons of life. Newlyweds soon learn that what started out as moonlight and roses soon turns to daylight and dishes. Couples with young children are among the first to report that the bedroom has become the dull room. When children come into the home, romance can easily go out. Leisurely evenings by the stereo give way to trips to the playground. Late nights once spent in each other's arms are now consumed by comforting a sick or restless child. When couples lack time together, their lovemaking is reduced to quick physical encounters to release pent-up passion.

Not only will we need to plan for our lovemaking sessions; we may, when we are busy, have to schedule them. Some people resist this because they think that sex should be spontaneous and that it should certainly not be work. I'm not suggesting that you use your Day-Timer to schedule sexual intercourse, but I am suggesting that you plan for time alone and activities that might lead to sex: candlelight dinners, walks, weekends away, and all sorts of romantic activities suggested in earlier chapters. Unless you budget some time for sex play, the crush of everyday activities could crowd it out.

Try Something Different

You'll also want to vary your lovemaking times, variety being, as it is, the spice of life. Novelty seems necessary to sustain the intensity of your physical relationship. It's too easy to get into a rut, lovemaking becoming routine. Observes one expert, "In a long-term relationship, people usually learn the most efficient ways to turn each other on—and then it gets boring after a while."[14] "Try something different," advises one counselor. "You wouldn't want to eat the same thing every day, no matter how delicious it is, or watch the same movie over and over."

If God has given us our bodies and our partners to pleasure each other, why should we shy away from being creative? Obviously, sex acts that involve other people or that are abusive are out of bounds. Some Christians frown on what one calls "freaky sex,"[15] censuring certain diversions because they claim these acts are unnatural. But who is to judge what is natural or not? Lips, mouths, and tongues are sensitive erogenous zones.

According to one commentator, oral sex may even be mentioned in the Song of Songs, where the woman says of her lover: "Like an apple tree among the trees of the forest is my lover among the young men. I delight to sit in his shade, and his fruit is sweet to my taste" (Song 2:3).

Of this passage Jody Dillow writes, "In extra-biblical literature, 'fruit' is sometimes equated with the male genitals or with semen, so it is possible that here we have a faint and delicate reference to an oral genital caress."[16] The highly figurative language of this passage makes it difficult to be sure this is what it means, as Dillow admits. His "fruit" may simply symbolize the man's sexual caresses.

Let Meaning Be Your Guide

If we think holistically about sex, being creative about it makes sense. That is, whatever we do is done with purpose. In this sense, within moral limitations, the end can justify the means. Perhaps a certain position simply increases the physical intensity, so we drive each other wild, as many magazine articles recommend. But to increase the joys of sex play we must aim for pleasure that is more than physical. Instead, we should combine the erotic with love, intimacy, and all the other qualities of a committed, soulful relationship.

A husband might think his wife's suggestion is disgusting; she thinks it's intimate. Seeking variety is not merely attempting to do new things but to do meaningful things. In the side-by-side position of intercourse, for instance, a couple may feel more like intimate friends who are lying together in prolonged union, leisurely pleasuring each other with slow movements and deep eye contact. For some couples, oral sex can be an exceptional form of intimacy.

Asking if something is fun is not enough; we should ask if it makes us feel close, loved, together, cared for, valued, or affirmed. There are thousands of ways to experience these incredible feelings. Sex becomes an art form whenever couples inventively make love meaningfully. As artists fashion exquisite creations from pieces of driftwood, bits of yarn, or matchsticks, so couples create rapturous collages of love and intimacy out of nothing but themselves. This artistry requires releasing the child in us. We become like the little child who brings the dandelion to his mother; the mother sees it as a gift of his love. In a similar way, a sensual act is a creative gift of ourselves. As the child delights in frolicking through a field, so we delight in running our fingers through each other's hair. We are searching for simple, childlike ways of saying, "I love you, I want you, I desire to be close to you."

A good sex manual, such as Doug Roseneau's *Celebration of Sex,* describes all sorts of techniques to excite your imagination. To practice them, you will have to see the profound possibilities in the rather profane instructions. Mechanical directions like "put your leg here" or "place your hand there" might embarrass some readers. But following such mundane guidelines can yield new wonders.

Technique is not the only way to enrich your love life. A change of place can make a major difference, as the "better in the Bahamas" commercial suggests. It is a well-known fact that staying in a motel turns on most people. A motel or hotel provides the basic essentials for great romantic love. It gives privacy (we're alone to dress and undress as we like; we feel there's no one else in the world but us); freedom (to yell, moan, play, laugh within); uninterrupted time and space (no demanding doorbell or phone or children screaming for help); novelty (different colors, odors, feel of chairs and bed); leisure and rest (housework and cooking are left behind); and freedom from care (distance from daily concerns).

You can turn your bedroom into a similar setting. Make it sensually exciting, and put a lock on the door. You can't keep your children from yelling at you outside the door, but you can keep them from bursting into your room. There's novelty to be found in other places as well: another room in the house, outdoors, a tent, a car, or in the sauna or the shower. Aids such as scented oil, flowers, ice cubes, and the like can provide a sensual treat.

Also change the context. Surround yourself with music, bask in the light of candles or colored lights, read love poems to each other. For years one of the assignments my students could choose to do with their spouses was to read aloud the Song of Songs to each other. One man laughingly reported that he and his wife had tried it twice, but they were never able to get to the end.

You can vary what you wear or don't wear; sexy lingerie is not the only option. At the right moment a plain white T-shirt can pack a lot of erotic power.

Changing the pace of any sexual activity can be mind-blowing: build layer by layer the arousal, then plateau and start again, slow, then fast, then back to slow again.

Touch and movement too can be varied for great effect: stroking soft, then hard, back and forth, then in a circle; fondling an earlobe; using fingertips or nails. Women tend to like slow, gentle touches and circular motions; men tend to prefer harder, straight, and faster ones.

Words provide opportunities for endless novelty and surprise. Suggestive, seductive, and subtle ones are especially exciting. Note the woman's passionate request of her love: "Sustain me with raisin cakes, refresh me with apples, for I am faint with love" (Song 2:5). Note his poetic expression of desire: "You have stolen my heart, my sister, my bride; you have stolen my heart with one of your eyes. . . . How much more pleasing is your love than wine" (Song 4:9–10). Consider all the sensual nuances of a wife whispering to her husband at a party, "I'm not wearing any underwear," or a man leaving his wife a note about his plans for the evening.

Discover Each Other's Pleasure Points

To play any instrument you must first get acquainted with it. It would seem just as obvious that performing sexually requires knowing about your partner's body, especially the pleasure points called the erogenous zones. It's not my purpose to explain all there is to know about these; a complete sex manual will provide the details, clarified by diagrams and pictures. But I'll make a few suggestions.

Locate your own. Get to know your own pleasure zones. It's important to know what feels good so that you can tell your partner, who can then know how to pleasure you. Concentrate on what is happening to you physically during all phases of your lovemaking: the foreplay, sex play, intercourse, orgasm, and afterwards (called the resolution phase). You will also try to learn from your partner's words and actions what is happening to him or her. Then recognize how you and your partner are similar. But we can also learn a lot about the opposite sex by recognizing how much alike men and women are.

Recognize the similarities. Despite their glaring differences, male and female genitals have many similarities. Studies of how a human embryo develops show that the different genitals originated in about the same places on the body. The head of a woman's clitoris develops from the same tissue that the head of the penis does. This little head of the clitoris (called a glans, as is the head of a penis) even has a foreskin around it. When a woman is aroused, this glans enlarges and pokes out of its hood. Stroking and touching it causes the same sensations in a woman as stroking the head of a penis creates in a man. If he knows this, a husband can easily determine that his wife will enjoy having done to her whatever he would enjoy having done to him.

The woman also has a shaft similar to that of the penis. Hers lies under the outer lips of the vagina, at the top. It points downward, with the head of the clitoris attached at the lower end. As does the penis, this shaft becomes stiff when it is engorged with blood during arousal. It too, when it's touched like the penis shaft, accounts for waves of electric sensation. Whatever a woman can do to a man's penis, a man can do to a woman's clitoris with the same effect. Other parts also are made of the same tissue and have the same sensitivity. The underside of the penis corresponds to the vulva's inner lips, which are rich in nerve endings.

It's clear then that the clitoris plays a major part in a woman's orgasm, as does the penis in a man. It's helpful to understand that even an orgasm is much the same for both men and women. It is rather special to understand that at that moment you are sharing the same sensations; though a man experiences ejaculation, he also has an orgasm that is similar to his wife's. During climaxing, for both men and women, the muscles surrounding the anus and genitals force the blood from the pelvic area, which was engorged with it during arousal. Because these muscles play a major role in sexual intercourse, the regular exercise of them can enhance the pleasure of both partners. A woman can use the strengthened muscles to tighten her vagina. The so-called Kegel exercise, which is named after a physician, can be done at any time. Muscles in the region are tightened (as if cutting off the flow of urine) ten times; count to two or three each time. Doing this periodically throughout the week keeps the muscles in tone.

Many of the husband's and wife's erogenous zones are the same: earlobes, behind the ears, underarms, nipples, sides of the breasts, lower abdomen, pubic area, vulva and pelvic area, the buttocks, the anus and the area around it, inner thighs, behind the knees, feet, and toes. Some of the pleasure spots are different; the perineum, or the area between a man's anus and scrotum, and the so-called G-spot of a woman are both sensitive. The G-spot is on the front wall of the vagina, a few inches inside. Fingers curled toward the belly will reach it, as will sexual intercourse from behind.

TUNE IN TO YOUR TURN-ONS

One of the keys to selecting any variation is knowing your turn-ons as well as those of your partner. Sex therapist Jack Morin calls these our erotic themes and claims that most couples are not fully aware of them. Yet these erotic themes create and sustain our passion. Most of us know what sensual activity we prefer, but we may not know why we do. Once we answer that question, we can expand our lovemaking repertoire by doing other things that produce the same effect.

A woman in one of my seminars related that her most memorable lovemaking session with her husband took place on a lonely road in the backseat of a car. This was after they had been married for more than forty years. Why was this so monumental? Perhaps it was the novelty; she needed something different, and she got it. Or it may have signified being young again, since a romp in a sedan is something twenty-year-olds would do, and the youthfulness of it aroused her passions to a new level. Or the erotic theme perhaps was being naughty, since backseats and lovers' lanes are associated with being promiscuous. Maybe it was simply the playfulness that heated up the car that night. There is yet another plausible explanation: danger turned her on. Though the road was lonely, there was still the possibility of being caught in the act. It was perilous enough to arouse her though not enough to inhibit her. We cannot know for certain what erotic theme made this such a momentous occasion. But if this woman thought about it and used her discoveries to invent new ways, she might produce the same effect.

We can do the same by analyzing our peak experiences. They will tell us a lot about the sensual desires that lie deep within our personality, revealing an enormous amount about how our eroticism works.[17] Morin suggests we ask certain questions as we think back on our most compelling turn-ons to determine what made them so special: the context, what you did, what was said, who did or said it. How did you feel: passionate, intimate, loved?

Another way to detect your erotic themes is by studying your fantasies since these arousal themes inspire the fantasies. As Christians, we might be suspicious of doing this, since we usually consider sexual fantasies taboo. Our minds are to be focused on whatever is true, noble, right, pure, lovely, and admirable (Phil. 4:8).

However, not all sexual fantasies are impure or ignoble. An erotic daydream that involves your spouse might not be. (By the way, most men say their wives are the objects of their fantasies.) Obviously, some of our fantasies need to be discarded: those that involve promiscuity or group sex or that focus on people other than our spouses. Yet even an unwholesome fantasy can teach us about our sensuality. We can analyze these fantasies even as we struggle to discard them. Stopping to think rationally about a fantasy will tend to destroy it.

If we ponder our fantasies, they may tip us off to what we really want in our marriage. For example, men commonly fantasize about being seduced by an aggressive, passionate, and uninhibited woman. At first glance, we may conclude that behind this is a sinful yearning to be promiscuous. However, underlying this could be any number of causes, among them a desire to have his masculinity affirmed or a yearning to be wanted.

A man wants a wife who enjoys making love, not one who merely wants to please him. He may be reluctant to take without giving something in return. From pondering this fantasy a husband might discover that he longs for his wife to be more aggressive and responsive. His wife may fantasize about being passive and having a man aggressively pursue her. Though her submissiveness is a turn-on for her, it is somewhat in conflict with her husband's desire for her sometimes to be the sexual aggressor. If they have the courage to share their fantasies or the themes behind them, they can create some pleasurable times together.

As I mentioned, we need to avoid playing out any improper turn-ons. A husband, for example, may daydream about being ravished by a woman because he requires this to bolster his excessively low self-esteem, but he may need to be careful not to nurture this. Instead, he needs to concentrate on ways to confirm his manhood other than by thinking of himself as being sexually attractive. While he should expect his physical relationship with his wife to provide some affirmation of who he is, he should not depend on it excessively.

Forbiddenness is another questionable theme. If being naughty made a frolic in the car special, a woman may not want to nurture that. All sorts of erotic themes fire deviant behavior that needs to be avoided: hurting (leading to sadistic acts), being punished (masochism), being humiliated, being rebellious, being dominated or dominating.

A Christian couple I counseled is an amazing example of how an erotic theme can so powerfully drive a person. This couple came to me because they were in the process of being reconciled after the thirty-some-year-old wife had an affair that lasted several years before her husband became aware of it. The strange, perplexing problem they asked about was this: after his wife's affair, the husband's sex with her was fantastic. Previously she had been unresponsive and unimpassioned in bed. Now their sex was torrid, fired by her initiating all sorts of lovemaking she had learned from her promiscuous lover. Also, the husband wanted help in dealing with his conflicting feelings of being glad for his wife's new responsiveness and the hurt caused by the source of that responsiveness.

After a lot of discussion, we concluded that the wife's sensual awakening was mostly prompted by her attitude toward sex as something forbidden. Though she felt guilty when she was having her affair, she was also turned on by it. The husband should not fault himself for her previous coolness toward sex, nor should her adulterous partner be credited for her new interest in it. These insights helped the husband to deal with the jealousy and pain he was feeling.

Since they both believed the affair was over and that they had been reconciled, I urged them to accept without reservation their newfound sensual fervor. That the wife was so sexually responsive to her husband indicated that a positive change had taken place in her. She was now aroused by being in love, not by being immoral.

Whatever you decide to do about any of your questionable erotic themes, it is wise to be aware of them. The worst approach is to ignore them. Morin explains, "Lusty urges are most affirming when they are woven into the fabric of everyday life. Conversely, lust is more likely to turn destructive when it is split off from the rest of life, banished to a dark corner, where it festers and grows hostile."[18]

Failing to recognize these passions and deal with them can lead to compulsively acting them out, something rapists, sadists, and the like are prone to do. Morin claims that their failure to deal with the root cause of their deviant arousal makes them unable to draw a clear line between fantasy and behavior. People who can't make that distinction may feel driven to make their fantasies a reality.

See Inside Yourself

Taking an honest look at your inner self is a major part of staying spiritually healthy. People who repress the dark side of themselves fail to repent adequately, which involves changing your mind about who you are. Jesus told us that the heart is the source of all sorts of wrongdoing: out of it "come evil thoughts, murder, adultery, sexual immorality, theft, false testimony, slander" (Matt. 15:19). The word *heart* in the Bible refers to the core of our being, including our feelings, attitudes, and thoughts.

Examining our heart and admitting what's there is part of the process of dealing with sin. The same is true in ridding ourselves of any unwanted turn-ons. We should try to identify them and then trace their origin. Morin maintains that they were bred in our childhood and are now the result of unresolved issues. A woman, for example, who turns on to being dominated may have been reared by a controlling father. Overly strict parents could have produced someone who is turned on by being naughty. Such parents could also cause a person to associate sex with rebellion and anger. In marriage this might prompt someone to be turned on by having a fight with a partner or fantasizing about cheating.

When you are seeking to play out proper erotic themes, you may need to do some courageous experimentation. We can't always wait until we feel like doing something before we try it. To change our conscience we may have to do things we feel guilty about, or we may need to act even if our heart isn't in it. Sometimes our actions have to change before our attitude does. Recall how you felt when you were lounging by a swimming pool and absorbing the sunshine. You heard someone scream at you to come into the water. Every fiber of your relaxed, warm body said "no way." You couldn't imagine giving up your warm place in the sun for a plunge into cold water. Yet after coaxing or perhaps a little tugging, you found yourself in the pool. After a few minutes you were relishing it. The same is true of our lovemaking. What our spouse invites us to do may not be appealing at first. But if we do cooperate, convinced in our minds it's OK, after awhile our conscience will be convinced as well.

MAKE HASTE SLOWLY

Of course the change won't always be instant; it may take time. Enriching your love life will require patience with yourself as well as with your partner. Talk over ways to improve; try new things. If you can't always be frank about what you want, try being subtle. When you are making love, a simple request will do: "Put your hand there," "Move more this way," "Let's try this." Expand your repertoire as you are able, without pushing too far past your comfort zone. We should be careful not to force our partners to do what embarrasses or offends them.

Over time lovers change, enjoying things later in marriage they couldn't enjoy earlier. Seasoned lovers prove what one expert says: "When it comes to sex, practice really does make perfect."[19] A study done by the American Association of Retired People found that older couples in general were enjoying the best sex of their lives. Years of experience and a matured marriage relationship apparently have made them into ecstatic lovers.

Partners eager to do new things must make haste slowly. This is especially crucial for the husband to do since a woman may be more reluctant than a man to be sensually daring. Perhaps the Song of Songs is hinting that this is the nature of a woman: her sensuality is like a garden locked up (Song 4:12). Any fences of restraint might not always be removed quickly. A husband can unlock her passions, but it may take time; and it is well worth it. Love works in a thousand different ways. Why not try them all?

🙢 *Pillow Talk* 🙢

PLEASURE PLANNING

This sharing game is designed to proceed slowly, since this kind of exchange can be rather touchy. Proceed only as far as you both agree to go.

Step 1: Using small cards or slips of paper, each of you makes two stacks of items under the following labels. You can use the following examples as a guide. Attempt to be frank but kind.

What I Like About Our Sexual Relationship
Husband
- I like it when you are extremely excited and turned on.
- I love it when you dress up in a special, sexy way.
- I like it when you suggest turning on the music.
- I like it when you signal a need for sex by having a candlelight dinner, etc.
- I like it when you are on the top and insist on staying there.
- I like it when your hands go roving all over.
- I like what oral sex we do have, especially when you are in the mood for it.

What I Wish About Our Sexual Relationship
Husband
- I wish you would talk more during our lovemaking.
- I wish you would actually initiate our lovemaking and aggressively guide the whole process once in awhile.
- I wish you wouldn't always want to take so long before we reach orgasm.
- I wish we would have oral sex more often and that it would be both ways.
- I wish you would increase the number of signals you give whenever you want me or even learn to say so.

What I Like About Our Sexual Relationship
Wife
- I like it when you take me out for an evening of fun and romance as a prelude.
- I like you to hold me in your arms and kiss me for a long time in a room other than the bedroom, like we did when we were first married.
- I like it when you get turned on by what I am wearing.
- I like you to wear colored underwear because I know you are doing it for me.
- I like lots of foreplay, especially before we take off our clothes.

What I Wish About Our Sexual Relationship
Wife

- I wish we would have more romantic moments more often.
- I wish I could enjoy oral sex more than I do but wish you wouldn't push me in this area.
- I wish you would make sure you have shaved before our love-making since the roughness of your beard seems to distract me.
- I wish you would spend more time in foreplay.
- I wish you would touch my breasts more lightly at first.
- I wish you would wait until I am more excited and enthusiastic before suggesting new positions; I don't feel good about refusing you.
- I wish you would tell me how you feel whenever something goes wrong during our lovemaking. You end it abruptly and then seem to roll away without my understanding you.

Step 2: You now have four stacks of cards before you. Shuffle each stack, keeping them separate.

1. Begin by having each of you taking a card from the other's pile of "What I Like" items. Read it out loud. Comment by saying either "I knew that" or "I never knew that." Then explain and discuss.

2. Next, each of you should take a card or slip from the other's stack of "What I Wish" items. Here you should decide not to argue but rather attempt to understand each other's expectations and desires.

Read the card out loud. First you should discuss it until you can say, "I understand what you mean." Then comment by saying, "I knew that" or "I never knew that." Then explain and discuss.

3. Continue by alternating from the "What I Like" to the "What I Wish" items, ending the session whenever either of you desires to stop. Items may be kept for another session.

Chapter Seven

SEX AND PREVENTION

DELIVERING US FROM EVIL

*T*he depression displayed in his downcast eyes along with his soft, slow speech betrayed the smile he was forcing to cover it up. "Pray for me," he asked. "The temptation is fierce." He feared what his burning sexual passion—passion that was not spent in his marriage because of his sexually unresponsive wife—might drive him to do.

Jesus taught us to pray daily, "Lead us not into temptation" (Matt. 6:13). For many of us, the temptations we face daily, if not hourly, are sexual ones. In *Eros Defiled,* John White vividly described them:

> Some of us are full of sexual urges, urges with which we wish we did not have to cope. How then can we in the twentieth century, stimulated artificially every day in a score of ways, be in control of our passions?[1]

A BIBLICAL ANSWER: MARRIAGE DELIVERS

In the first century, the apostle Paul proposed an answer. For those who burned with lust, he advised marrying, then maintaining a satisfying sex life. His words comprise the most explicit passage on marital sex in the Bible. After approving, even commending, singleness, he said, "But since there is so much immorality, each man should have his own wife, and each woman her own husband" (1 Cor. 7:2). Once people are married, he continued, "The husband should fulfill his marital duty to his wife, and likewise the wife to her husband" (1 Cor. 7:3); married people have a sexual obligation to each other. In fact, Paul made a rather radical statement: "The wife's body does not belong to her alone but also to her husband. In the same way, the husband's body does not belong to him alone but also to his wife" (1 Cor. 7:4).

Essentially, Paul prescribes marital sex as a vaccine against illegitimate sex. Calling this the Pauline principle, all theologians have affirmed the purifying role of the marriage bed. Augustine listed it as one of the purposes of marriage, justifying the physical relation between married partners even though he considered sex disgustingly unspiritual. Yet Paul converts what some theologians consider a carnal activity into a spiritual one. For Christians, marital sex is a moral duty.

I've deliberately chosen to discuss this purpose last because for so many years it was made first, at least for women. The bed was an altar where they sacrificially submitted themselves to their masters. Their sense of duty was the only reason they reluctantly engaged in sex, especially when conceiving a child was not involved. Any enjoyment in the marital bed was to be found in giving, not receiving, and this resulted in the neglect of their own sensual pleasure.

But Paul was not so callous about a woman's need for passion. Husbands are as obligated to satisfy their wives as wives are to pleasure husbands. "The husband's body does not belong to him alone but also to his wife" (1 Cor. 7:4). The literal translation of the Greek is even more forceful: "The woman has authority over the man's body." Paul was far more sexually liberated in his thinking than many people give him credit for. That the apostle Paul was such a spiritual man makes his remedy for temptation even more remarkable. We might have expected that a man who performed miracles, saw visions, and ministered with supernatural power would advise long prayers and cold showers. Yet he is so down-to-earth that he cautions couples not to abstain from sex for too long a time. And if they do, both must agree to do so. "Do not deprive each other except by mutual consent and for a time, so that you may devote yourselves to prayer. Then come together again so that Satan will not tempt you because of your lack of self-control" (1 Cor. 7:5).

Paul's allusion to marriage as a substitute for burning is an apt one. Regular sexual relations quench the heated passions that, in James's words, drag us away and entice us to sin (James 1:14). Marital sex cleanses us, morally and spiritually. It flushes from our minds the sensual thoughts and images that collect there during the day, often without our consent. When he wrote to the Corinthians, Paul probably was thinking of passages from the Old Testament, which take the same approach to marital sex. To avoid infidelity, husbands are told to concentrate on their wives' sensuality, symbolized by water, in order to avoid infidelity. "Drink water from your own cistern, running water from your own well. Should your springs overflow in the streets, your streams of water in the public squares? Let them be yours alone, never to be shared with strangers. May your fountain be blessed, and may you rejoice in the wife of your youth" (Prov. 5:15–18).

Instead of being lured to immorality, husbands were to lust only for their wives. "Why be captivated, my son, by an adulteress? Why embrace the bosom of another man's wife?" (Prov. 5:20). The meaning of this question is even more poignant if the word *captivated* is translated "captured," as it also can be. God says that a man is to be captured by his wife so that he won't be captured by an adulteress. Note too that the reference is to the wife of a man's youth, not a youthful wife, suggesting a man's passion for his wife should not wane as she grows older. This is especially important because we live so much longer than did people who lived when this Scripture was written. The rate of life expectancy being as it is, most couples can expect to be together for forty-five years or more. This is all the more reason they need to keep their lovemaking fresh in all of life's seasons.

What is said of husbands in Proverbs 5 is also true of wives. A wife's love is symbolized as a private water reservoir and spring. A husband is told to drink from these. Otherwise their water will overflow in the streets, which is a reference to a wife's promiscuity. A husband's sexual devotion to his wife, like hers to him, reduces the chance of adultery.

We place our partner in moral peril if we neglect our love life. Pent-up sexual desires increase the risk of adultery. When people let sex go out of their marriage, they often go out of their marriage for sex. For this reason it is drastically wrong to suggest, as some people in the past have, that it is spiritually beneficial to disregard sex. It is more spiritual for a couple to indulge in it.

ADULTERY AND ITS CONSEQUENCES

Paul, unlike other Christian leaders throughout the history of the church, says nothing about repressing sex. Such a dim view of sex within marriage often fosters it elsewhere. In the Middle Ages, sexual sins were so common that they weren't taken seriously, as one historian observed: "Confess them to the priest, and for a few routine prayers and a small cash contribution, he could release them from your spiritual record."[2]

It was common and acceptable for a man to have a mistress. In some historical periods even clerics and popes had mistresses. Plentiful evidence shows it was grossly more sinful for a priest to marry than it was for him to have a mistress. In the popular literature of the thirteenth century, clerical celibacy was a joke.[3] During the twelfth century in Spain, it was acceptable for a young bachelor to keep a *barrangana* (mistress) until he was ready for marriage. Priests in Spain and elsewhere did the same. "Everyone who entered the clergy made a vow of chastity," claims one historian, "but almost none observed it."[4]

Adultery is a perilous road to travel; its destination extremely dangerous, spiritually and practically. God's warnings about extramarital sex are not just the whims of a powerful deity who wants to take fun out of our lives. The Book of Proverbs gives a graphic picture of the ruinous consequences of adultery.

Adultery promises poverty and physical harm. Much of the ruin is described in terms of death. The promiscuous woman's "feet go down to death; her steps lead straight to the grave" (Prov. 5:5). Although she promises a feast with sweet water and delicious food, in reality the dead are in her house and "her guests are in the depths of the grave" (Prov. 9:18). The prostitute's path leads "to the spirits of the dead. None who go to her return or attain the paths of life" (Prov. 2:18–19).

Sex has the power to destroy lives and bring down the mighty: "Many are the victims she has brought down; her slain are a mighty throng. Her house is a highway to the grave, leading down to the chambers of death" (Prov. 7:26–27).

These are sobering thoughts in an age when we can flick a switch and see actors on the daily soaps playing their games of musical beds. When the charming actor follows the shapely actress to her bedroom, there is no feeling for the tragic outcome. "All at once he followed her like an ox going to the slaughter, like a deer stepping into a noose till an arrow pierces his liver, like a bird darting into a snare, little knowing it will cost him his life" (Prov. 7:22–23). Our novels and films rarely portray the diseases of the body and the wounds to the soul. Instead, like the wayward wife of Proverbs, they scream to us, "Come . . . let's enjoy ourselves with love!" (Prov. 7:18). Rarely do they tell us that "the adulteress preys upon your very life" (Prov. 6:26).

It's easy to lose sight of this, as it was for a divorced woman who sought my help. She was slowly becoming involved with a married man. The affair started with casual glances in church. Seeing him privately and hearing of his affection for her was drawing her close to a sexual encounter with him. She was startled not because it was happening but because it seemed so harmless. "When he tells me how attractive I am, I feel excited and wonderful. When I'm with him, I'm so happy." How could something so good be so bad? That was the question that bothered her.

Whether a woman or a man is the initiator, the Proverbs portray the affair as a mixture of good and bad. "For the lips of an adulteress drip honey, and her speech is smoother than oil; but in the end she is bitter as gall, sharp as a double-edged sword" (Prov. 5:3–4). Part of the damage of unfaithfulness is shame. It is said of the man who commits adultery: "Blows and disgrace are his lot, and his shame will never be wiped away" (Prov. 6:33). Shame occurs for both the man and the woman, eroding their self-esteem.

Others also suffer from a person's infidelity. Paul speaks of adultery with another man's wife as wronging a brother (1 Thess. 4:6). Proverbs 12:4 may be the most direct description of what the unfaithful woman does to her husband: "A disgraceful wife is like decay in his bones." Rottenness slowly spreading through the skeleton may symbolize the inner emotional pain a wounded spouse feels. Seducing another person's spouse injures that person. Betrayed spouses sometimes require long hours of counseling or even institutionalized care to recover from the hurt. Children of the wandering parent are also emotionally damaged, some severely.

MARRIAGE AS A PUBLIC HEALTH MESSAGE

Several years ago in our faculty lounge, some of the other professors and I were discussing the news that Jim Fixx, author of two major books about jogging, had died of a heart attack while he was running. Someone then mentioned that Euell Gibbons, who had penned books about eating wild herbs, had died of a stomach ailment. I jokingly blurted out, "Oh, I wrote a book about sex and marriage."

Our awareness of AIDS means that we know extramarital sex can be fatal. But the public is not as informed about other health hazards of sex. The Medical Institute for Sexual Health reports that sexually transmitted diseases (STDs) are at an epidemic rate in the United States. A 1998 report of sexually active women at Rutgers University showed that 60 percent of them tested positive for human papillomavirus (HPV) at some time during the three-year study. HPV is a disease that infects an estimated 5.5 million Americans each year. It causes nearly all cases of cervical cancer, which annually causes the death of approximately five thousand American women and 250,000 women worldwide. In addition, a 1997 study of genital herpes found that one in five Americans over the age of eleven shows evidence of genital herpes infection (and 45.9 percent of African Americans over age eleven show evidence). Other studies indicate that if an individual has herpes or certain other sexually transmitted diseases, that person is three to five times more likely to become HIV-infected if a subsequent sexual partner has HIV/AIDS.[5]

Experience confirms that Paul is correct: marriage can be an antidote to immorality. Reporting recent research, the Medical Institute for Sexual Health concludes, "Marriage is a legitimate and powerful public health message." It is the relationship where the most frequent and pleasurable sex occurs as well as the environment that most strongly protects sexually active individuals from sexually transmitted diseases.[6]

Recent studies of the frequency of mates cheating on their partners do not show that high numbers of spouses are unfaithful, as some studies in the past have suggested. Because of a famous research study done in 1948, it has been common to say that 50 percent of married men cheat on their wives.[7] More accurate rates are 37 percent for men and 20 percent for women, making the authors of the recent *Sex in America* report more positive about American marriages: "About 90 percent of Americans have married by the time they are 30 and a large majority spends much of their adulthood as part of a wedded couple. And marriage, we find, regulates sexual behavior with remarkable precision." No matter what they did before they wed, no matter how many partners they had, the sexual lives of married people are similar. Most people are faithful while the marriage is intact. Once they are married, the vast majority of individuals have no other sexual partner.[8]

After analyzing two Gallup surveys and other studies, Andrew Greeley is even more positive about marriages. He discovered that about 91 percent of women and 89 percent of men say that they have had only one sexual partner for the duration of their present marriage. These percentages, he maintains, have been true for many years, not merely since the AIDS epidemic. Greeley comically calls it a fidelity epidemic. "True, there's more divorce than in the past; but, there's not much more infidelity."[9]

This view of marital faithfulness is different from the everybody's-doing-it notion the media often present. And it offers us the hope that our own marriage can be affair-free. If we have a good marital and sexual relationship, we can help to keep each other faithful. Sizable numbers of people who do stray say they didn't concentrate on a good marital relationship.

SHARE LOVINGLY

Because marital sex keeps us from sin, we owe it to each other. It's a spiritual obligation. There should be no strings attached to sex within marriage. Sex is not a favor to withhold. Sex is not a weapon to dominate. Sex is not a reward to be given for good behavior. Sex is not a payment to be earned.

I talk to many people who can't understand this; their own sexual desire is so scanty that they can't understand their partner's need. Many of them try hard to fulfill their duty, and I've heard them talk of their frustration. But I also know of those who have become bitter and indifferent to their partner's sexual needs. The least they can do is seek help for whatever sexual dysfunction they have. Sexual therapy is more available and more effective than ever.

Two questions regarding meeting a partner's sexual needs nearly always are asked during our marriage seminars. Should a wife who is not aroused submit to her husband to relieve his sexual need? Is sexual intercourse the only acceptable way to do this?

The first question hardly seems to be an issue with Christian couples with whom we've talked. Women are willing to do this for their husbands, especially since most men want sex more often than their wives do. Charlie Shedd's wife calls it a ministry to him, and it seems that this is in keeping with Paul's suggestion.

Using other means to satisfy each other is not so readily accepted by all couples. Though in earlier chapters I've urged that we celebrate freedom and creativity in the bedroom, this issue calls for further discussion. Counselor John White, without any sufficient basis, claims that anything other than intercourse should be used only along with it and never as a substitute. He approves of other means as foreplay and sex play, but every sexual encounter, he says, should end in intercourse. This seems to be unfair to the wife and rather impractical, since an unaroused husband cannot meet his wife's need for intercourse, as she can for him. Besides, many wives, especially early in marriage, may have a difficult time climaxing via intercourse, needing manual stimulation to the clitoris to do so.

If we follow Paul's principle, it would seem reasonable for a husband, if on occasion he is unable to have an erection, to minister to his wife in other ways. Most men are aware of ways to satisfy an impassioned woman other than genital intercourse. In a recent study of the love lives of senior citizens done by the American Association of Retired People, people reported that their sexual repertoire includes far more than genital sex.

Centuries ago this issue was addressed in Roman Catholic confessional instructions. "If the husband should withdraw after ejaculation, before the wife has experienced orgasm, she may lawfully at once continue friction with her own hand, in order to attain relief."[10]

Numerous women have asked us if it was right for them to have sex with husbands who show absolutely no affection for them outside the bedroom. "He's only interested in my body," they say. Feeling used, their resentment drives these wives to strike back by holding out. However, if we are to listen to Scripture, these women should not stop offering themselves to their husbands. A wife's body is a husband's to "use," and of course, his is also hers. Though using each other in this way is not the best reason for making love, it is one of them. And it may be the one bond that keeps the marriage together and eventually leads to a better one. This is part of the sacrificial nature of the marriage relationship. Men are to be willing not only to die for their wives but also to live sacrificially for them, caring for them as for their own bodies. This translates into regarding her sexual needs as well as his own.

Paul's statement about our obligation to each other should not be misused. It doesn't give us the right to expect sex on demand. Many women have told Ginger and me that their husbands use this passage to persuade them to do sexual things they aren't ready for. This is contrary to the spirit of love that should be a major part of sexual sharing. Just as we should not be reluctant in our giving of sex, we should not be unkind in our asking for it. We should seduce, not force, one another.

Making unreasonable demands may be a sign that sex has become an obsession, though it's not always easy to determine when a problem exists. When it comes to sex, people have different ideas of what is normal. Some people insist a spouse is oversexed if once a week isn't satisfying. In this case, the accusers are, statistically speaking, mistaken, because normally it's two to three times that. Some people, however, do fall outside any normal range and become a serious problem to their spouses and to themselves.

STAYING SENSUALLY SANE IN A SEX-CRAZED SOCIETY

Such a fixation on sex is partly due to living in a society that is saturated with sensual images, just as Corinth was in Paul's day. Corinth was the scene of the extremes of the Roman Empire's moral decadence. In this major cosmopolitan center, cavorting with a temple prostitute was a religious act. People were encased in sensuality, and temptation was intense.

So it is for us, especially in the United States. The media—television, magazines, books, billboards, videos, and the Internet—constantly call our attention to sex. So do provocatively dressed men and women, clubs and bars with X-rated dancers, and adult shops. Couples must cope with this constant barrage, especially pornography. Its availability at the click of a mouse button has made pornography a major temptation for many people. Pornography is also a multibillion-dollar industry; not only is there more of it, but what is available is far more decadent than ever before. Some ethicists warn we are fast becoming a shameless society, a fact that is eroding our moral foundation.

This fact is also corroding marriages, or at least disrupting them. Judy, for instance, became aware of an issue shortly after her wedding. Though her husband lavished plenty of sexual attention on her, he also did so elsewhere. Several times she caught him logged on to sexually explicit sites on the Internet. When she asked, he admitted he did masturbate periodically. Added to this, she spotted him taking more than a glance at women at church. She was facing what many newly married women face: a male's awesome preoccupation with sex. My guess is that this Christian couple is typical, though I have no research to prove it. For couples today, sex in the marketplace is as much an issue as sex in the bedroom.

Potential Issues

Spouses sometimes fret that their partner is being disloyal to them when they notice attractive members of the opposite sex. Women are especially disturbed when they see their husband's head turned by a passing female. Also, as I mentioned in chapter 5, wives feel especially threatened by the pictures of shapely models and actresses that show up everywhere. Even the most attractive wives will have a difficult time competing with these women, who have the advantages of cosmetic alterations and photographic techniques. Besides, husbands see their wives at times when they look their worst. Husbands face the same threat since their wives are exposed to handsome, appealing images of the male species. Men are likely to hear women, their wives among them, ooh and aah about buns and abs.

A second issue is the impact of this glut of carnality on our spiritual lives. "But they are only pictures" is often used as a justification for dabbling in pornography. But the images are powerful and linger in the mind, obviously distracting, possibly destructive. Whoever said the mind is a battleground was right. The fight for purity begins there; and to think on whatever is noble, whatever is pure, whatever is lovely is not easy. Not only must we guard our own minds, but also we may wonder how well our partners are guarding theirs.

The third concern is that looking and thinking may lead to lusting and doing. Married persons' worst fear is that constant exposure to this parade of sensuality may lead their spouses to become unfaithful or become obsessed with sex. Many psychologists maintain that people become hooked on sex in the same way that they become hooked on drugs. Whether or not this should be called an addiction, sex does seem to become an extreme fixation for some people. A friend of mine who is a counselor in a large California church says that it is the fastest-growing problem among men, even among Christian men. Though using pornography will not always lead to addiction, it may contribute to it. A survey of sex addicts showed that 90 percent of the men and 77 percent of the women used pornography.[11]

Because the problem is new, people don't always suspect it's the cause of their marital distress. In my office, Terry, confused and depressed, described her husband's irresponsibility. For the first year of their marriage, he had been a model husband. After returning home from working in another city for several months, he showed little interest in his wife. Gone most evenings, he was rarely home with his wife and children. Rumors that he was having an affair with another woman were hard to believe of a man who claimed to be a Christian. Yet the fact that he rarely had sex with Terry seemed to confirm the rumor; so did the porn magazines she found hidden in the house. Despite her protests, as well as those of his Christian parents, he wouldn't or seemingly couldn't change his lifestyle. He seemed trapped. As it turned out, he was. The best explanation for this twenty-three-year-old man's radical decline from being a loving husband to an unfaithful one was sexual addiction.

Facing the Issues Together

In dealing with these matters, I don't intend to be dogmatic, since the issues are complex. Nor, for that same reason, will I say all that could be said about them. I offer these suggestions, with help from my wife, to provide some notions for you and your partner to discuss.

Noticing others of the opposite sex is the first matter. Such looking is done by both men and women, but men are much more apt to do it. And when they do, they are more likely to think sensual thoughts than are women. The average man is interested in sex. Archibald Hart's study of men who professed high moral standards makes that clear. Ninety-one percent of men reared in Christian homes had been exposed to pornography, compared with 98 percent of those from nonreligious homes.

Three of every five of them admitted they masturbate. Fifty-nine percent said they often or sometimes fantasized about having sex with someone other than their wife. When they were asked about how often they thought about sex, nearly 80 percent reported "daily" (one-fourth of these said "hourly").

To understand better what a man's looking means to him and to his partner, it is helpful to recognize there are different types of looking. Anyone can look at someone to admire him or her for various reasons. People are part of God's creation, beautiful in various ways. In the Bible some women are described as attractive or beautiful; some men are dubbed handsome. Someone had to notice.

Second, there is a glance that provokes sensual thoughts or arouses desires. Even these, though potentially a problem, may be innocent. Looking and thinking about sex are not exactly the same as willfully considering it. When Jesus said that looking at a woman lustfully is a form of adultery, the Greek phrase makes clear he was not referring to a passing glance but something beyond that. Jesus may have meant looking with the intention to seduce because adultery is committed in a man's heart when he makes a decision to pursue an illicit relationship. Or perhaps Jesus was referring to something less than that: a willful, calculated stare that arouses a man's sexual desire.

It would be radical for Jesus to equate thinking about sex as equivalent to adultery because it would allow no distinction between temptation and sin, as other Scripture does. James explains, "Each one is tempted when, by his own evil desire, he is dragged away and enticed. Then, after desire has conceived, it gives birth to sin, and sin, when it is full-grown, gives birth to death" (James 1:14–15). Being enticed is not sin; sin happens afterward. A man's head being turned and his thoughts being stirred by a seductive woman are not necessarily sinful. What he does later may be.

Psychologist James Dobson urges wives not to misunderstand and blame their husbands if they may not be too discriminating when it comes to what or who turns them on. A man, being visually oriented, thinks of sex when he sees a shapely female or a picture of a scantily clad one, whether or not the woman seems beautiful. He becomes aroused even if he doesn't know anything about the intelligence, personality, or background of the person occupying the body. Women, who are more discriminating, have a difficult time understanding this. Because of this difference, a wife may misinterpret a man's glance at another woman to mean he is dissatisfied with his wife. In reality he has probably not lost interest or displeased with her; he's just a man. His eyes are the major instrument of his arousal, just as they are when he looks at his wife. If he stops noticing other women, he will no longer notice her. Yet spouses should be sensitive to any uneasiness their glances may cause their partners. A man should go out of his way to assure his wife that she is attractive to him. He must help her understand that she is not a contestant in a Mrs. America pageant and he is not one of the judges. And if he were, he would not judge her on her weight, size, or physical attributes alone, but he would value her as a total person, one he selected and who continues to give him love that he delights in and treasures.

Husbands too will have to tolerate their wives being tempted in today's sensual climate, though her temptations may take a different form than his. She isn't as likely to be allured by *Playgirl* magazine, since pictures of nude males' bodies don't entice her as the image of a naked woman does her husband. This doesn't mean that nudity doesn't sexually arouse women; experiments reveal that they do have a physiological response to it, such as moistening. But these reactions are mostly unconscious. Consciously, less overtly erotic sights turn them on: eyes that show sincerity, a bald head that shows maturity, a hefty chest that signals strength. Also, fantasies arouse women—not the sexual kind like men's but the relational ones that are found in romance novels. Thus wives need to guard their minds, too, and use their understanding of their own temptations to empathize with their husbands' struggles in this area.

Being tempted to look lustfully at someone of the opposite sex is different from something more serious—deliberate leering. Ogling members of the opposite sex, whether in reality or virtual reality, is hazardous. The lust of the eyes does not come from the Father, says 1 John 2:16. Sensual images stick like Velcro to our minds, distracting us from our relationship to God and more wholesome activities. Using pornography also encourages its production. Then there's the potential guilt, shame, and erosion of self-esteem for anyone who can't avoid it. Besides all this, it's socially unhealthy for us to be in the habit of viewing people as sex objects and not as persons. Obviously an occasional lapse should not be considered a spiritual crisis. Sometimes curiosity rather than lust is involved. But a person who agonizingly gives in repeatedly may be in trouble—which leads us to the final two issues: adultery and sexual addiction.

Unbridled lust was Richard's problem. He began watching pornography films alone. Then he brought home videos for his wife to watch with him. Grudgingly, she joined him. Watching the films was then followed by hours of making love. It became more difficult for her as the videos he watched became more and more hard-core. Also, the sexual demands on her became obscenely excessive and frequent, often lasting many days in a row for hours at a time. Still, believing she should be submissive, she swallowed her disgust and consented. When sex took up so many afternoons and evenings that her husband neglected his work, she began to resist. They argued. Citing Bible verses to defend what he was doing, he accused her and evangelical Christians, which he himself claimed to be, of being puritanical and judgmental. His outbursts of anger included verbal abuse. Troubled and confused, she feared she was losing her mind. When the situation got even worse and he, during one quarrel, struck her, she turned to others for help.

Richard showed the major symptoms of sexual addiction. The misuse of sex had become his primary source of fulfillment, and he was unable to deal successfully with other relationships and responsibilities. That his condition had become progressively worse is also a major symptom, according to some experts. This is one of the most pernicious risks of involvement in any illegitimate sexual activity. Lust has the power to drive us further than we intended to go. Experts who study sexual addiction find that people go from viewing soft porn, to so-called hard porn, to phone sex, and then to promiscuous relationships.

Another sign, loss of control, is typical of any addiction. Even though they want to change, addicts can't seem to do so. Else why would some alcoholics, workaholics, and sexaholics repeat what is so damaging to them? For example, a Christian who pastored a suburban church was secretly picking up girls at downtown singles bars and having sex with them. His compulsion cost him his ministry, his reputation, and his marriage. Why would a person risk losing so much? We could ask this question of countless public figures. The only sensible answer for such senseless behavior is that their ability to control themselves is greatly impaired. That some people conquer their compulsion demonstrates that such people are not helpless. Yet they often appear to be.

Saying this may seem inconsistent with Scripture, which tells us we are responsible for our sin and no one should be considered helpless. But the idea of being out of control is also biblical. In Romans, Paul described sin as slavery. And other Scriptures speak of people being overtaken by sin and trapped. Some people get involved in wrongdoing that eventually overpowers them. Perhaps everyone struggles with one compulsion or another: eating chocolate, gossiping, being harshly judgmental, or working. Since these behaviors are not so obviously destructive as addictions to drugs, alcohol, sex, and the like, we may not think of these as addictions. But for some people they are. Only a relatively small percentage of people become addicted to destructive things (unless, of course, we include food or television in this category). Despite the alarm sounded over the heavy drinking at our colleges and universities, about 10 percent of drinkers become alcoholics. The rest choose to drink, even to excess, but they can stop when they see warning signs.

My guess is that the same thing is true of pornography. Most men can handle the temptation and guard themselves from it. Those susceptible to sexual addiction are those whose parents did not teach or model good behavior or who were unusually inconsistent in their parenting. So are those who were sexually abused as children, especially those involved sexually too early.[12] Anyone with great emotional pain and loneliness is at risk.

A husband or wife who is suspicious of a partner's sexual activity should take heed. Loved ones of addicts are just as prone to deny anything is wrong as are addicts themselves. Couples need to talk honestly about pornography and sexual addiction. If the situation seems serious, an addicted person should seek counseling and possibly help from a support group. Spouses of troubled persons should seek counseling or join a support group even if a partner is unwilling to do so. The counselor can help them cope with the addict as well as explain how they can intervene in the situation. They should not feel that a partner's sexual obsession or escapades are their fault, something the addict may try to make them believe. Blaming those closest to them for their problems is typical of addicts of all sorts.

Avoiding Undue Controlling

If our spouse's activities disturb us, we should let him or her know. Our opinions and feelings will help them discern if what they are doing is wrong. If you feel jealous and suspicious—though sometimes these emotions are uncalled for or excessive—this fact signals that something may be wrong. After voicing our concern, we should let our partner deal with the matter, not mistakenly trying to control his or her behavior. Manipulation, threats, nagging, and the like usually make matters worse, especially when addiction is involved. We should offer our support— encouraging, praying for, and listening to each other. If we feel responsible for controlling our partner's behavior, we may put ourselves in an impossible, frustrating situation.

Marriage is not a total oneness; the Hebrew word used in the phrase "one flesh" is a word for a composite oneness. When we are married, we still have our individuality, marriage being not like two scrambled eggs but like two eggs sunny-side up in a skillet. What a person believes or what she does with her time, as long as it doesn't interfere with fulfilling marriage duties, is up to that person. For instance, I know a man who forbids his wife to chew gum. That he insist she not chew it when they are kissing is fair. But to demand, as he does, that she not chew gum anytime is going too far. He's tramping on her private property, and that's trespassing.

Though it may be very difficult to do, I urge husbands and wives to have a frank discussion of how each is handling today's sexual temptation, especially the lure of pornography. One of my graduate students, a pastor in his late thirties had such a talk. It occurred when they were working on some assignments I had given to them. The husband gave me permission to share with you the following report.

My wife thought it was the best exercise so far. The statement that sparked our conversation was, "What I am afraid to talk about most. . . ." Several years ago we had a fairly open discussion on pornography, which had made me somewhat uncomfortable. She sensed that and so the last few years had shieded away from that topic. She didn't want to pry or be overly suspicious, but did wonder sometimes if this might be an area that I was struggling in. Some of it had to do with personal assurance that I was and would be faithful to her. I could reassure her that while I have had encounters with pornography occasionally in my life, it is not an on-going problem. She did not know why she was concerned, but that when she felt that way she decided to just pray for me, that I wouldn't be tripped up in that area of my life. I reassured her that I was committed to her and was not looking at pornographic materials. I think some of her fear involved the Internet and I usually keep the door of my office open; but I also explained to her that she could easily see what sites I had been at through the automatic recording device on the computer. She said she did not want to be suspicious and always looking over my shoulder, but felt a lot better after our discussion. I explained that guys are so visually oriented and being attracted to a woman might have nothing to do with love. It certainly does not mean there is anything wrong with the man's wife. My wife also knows that I have accountability with another pastor in town and a close lifelong friend, so she understands that some things I may discuss with them, than her. I would be afraid she would misunderstand some temptations I face and take them personally, as if there was something wrong with her. We both agreed the discussion was quite good.

BEING IN MARRIAGE BETTER THAN BEING IMMORAL

The best way to help our spouse avoid immorality, to return to Paul's suggestion, is by being a good sex partner. This doesn't mean competing with the appeal of sex in the marketplace on its own terms. Rather, we offer our spouses something different and better. Pornography, promiscuity, and the like epitomize the compartmentalization of sex I described in the first chapter. It is impersonal sex, sex stripped of its meaning. It leaves its users feeling empty and alone, erotically satiated but not emotionally satisfied. Nothing is left but to try to assuage their thirst by more mere erotic titillation that will leave them as hollow as before. This is why it is so dangerously progressive, dissatisfaction driving them to find more satis-faction, which never comes.

We have something much richer and satisfying to offer each other: a vigorous physical relationship in the context of a personal one. That is satisfying sex—great sex. This is because our greatest need and longing is not for sex. We can live and thrive without sex, but we can't live and thrive without love and intimacy and all the other things sex can and should convey. We should strive for sex with significance. That's the message of the Bible and of this book. Holistic sex is the real thing. Keep sense in your sensuality.

~ *Pillow Talk* ~
AGREEING TO DISAGREE

This Pillow Talk will probably be the most difficult one for you to do. The matters it deals with are both sensitive and controversial. Being willing to agree to disagree will help facilitate your discussion. When you are done, you should understand each other much better, and that's a great step forward.

Step 1: Read through the following items and decide together which you would like to discuss. You may want to put some aside for later, either because of time or because either of you is not comfortable in discussing them yet.

Step 2: Individually score the items you have chosen.

Step 3: Take one item at a time. Share your score, and then talk.

Agree	Somewhat Agree	Mildly Disagree	Disagree Strongly	Not Sure
1	2	3	4	5

1. Sex in marriage is an obligation and should be shared freely with each other.
2. Because the apostle Paul said that each partner has authority over the other person's body, partners should expect their partner to do anything sexually that they ask for.
3. Sex should be shared freely but not demanded.

4. In general, marriage does help people avoid promiscuous sex.

5. It is more spiritual to be a good sex partner in marriage than it is to abstain from sex.

6. Sexual intercourse with a spouse does tend to cleanse a person's mind of sexual thoughts.

7. If a person is unfaithful in marriage, it is because his or her partner was not sexually responsive.

8. People have affairs primarily because they are after sex, not a relationship.

9. A person can learn to become more interested in sex.

10. A husband or wife should have sex with each other even if one of them is not aroused.

11. Bringing a partner to a climax in ways other than intercourse is acceptable.

12. Women are as tempted as men to be promiscuous.

13. Looking at a person of the opposite sex and thinking about having sex with him or her is a sin.

14. Defining pornography is complex and difficult.

15. It is possible to become addicted to sex.

16. The danger of involvement in pornography leading to sexual addiction is very great.

17. Married partners should be careful not to try to control their partners too much.

18. It is best for married people to hold each other accountable only in areas that relate to their marriage.

19. Husbands and wives should not depend on each other to control their behavior but should work on their own self-discipline.

20. Husbands and wives should not allow their partner to depend on them to control their behavior, but instead, they should support their partner in exercising self-discipline.

Conclusion

SEXUAL ADJUSTMENT

IN THEIR WORDS

*T*he key to our lovemaking, as we have shown, lies in our attitudes toward sex. We have proposed that a healthy perspective results from recognizing the God-given aims of sex as well as their implications for our relationship. Essentially, we're suggesting you enrich all aspects of your marriage by asking and creatively answering a number of questions. If the purpose of sex is to express love, how can we make it more loving? If intimacy is its goal, what can we do sexually to feel closer to each other? And, if for strengthening our self-esteem, what will do that? If it's for pleasure, how can we make it more enjoyable? If regular lovemaking protects us from giving in to immorality, how can we make sure it does that? This approach can counter any negative attitudes we have toward sex. It makes it difficult to think of our erotic act as ugly or dirty when it makes such a beautiful contribution to our total relationship.

From the survey of some of our students, we found that, after marriage, most of them needed to deal with bad feelings toward sex.

These came from a variety of sources: childhood background, premarital sexual experiences, lack of information, exposure to dirty sex via the media, their acquaintances, and pornography.

BEDROOM BARRIERS

They reported a number of typical barriers to adjusting sexually. These obstacles ranged from simple first-night issues to more serious long-term matters.

A honeymoon surprise that troubled one woman was how messy sex was. "I didn't anticipate the amount of seminal fluid released, plus the lubricant." During their first night, a woman got angry with her husband when "he laughed out loud when he had his orgasm."

Anxiety about their bodies or shame were issues for some. "I had a hard time being naked in front of my husband and having a light in the room when having sex. It made me feel uncomfortable."

Feeling guilty about sex was not a problem for most of the couples, but it was for some. Wrote one, after several years of marriage, "I've begun to view sex as dirty and animal-like."

Others told of lack of communication, physical discomfort, each with different sex drives, not knowing what was normal, and severe conflict that interfered with their physical intimacy.

ELEMENTS OF AN EFFECTIVE FORMULA

Any of these problems can be overcome; our couples told us how they did so. Taken together, their approaches make an effective formula for cultivating our love life.

Be aware of what sex means to your marriage. More than 80 percent of those surveyed articulated clearly that recognizing the broader purposes of sex was the major factor in their improved sex lives.

Most noted that Scripture enabled them to discard any adverse attitudes toward sex by providing this broader meaning. One expressed it well: "I was raised in a reserved family. Sex, as well as many other topics, was not talked about. I still got a general picture about sex in class and in books, but this was biological. To me sex and things related to it were dirty, indecent, and shameful. Now I view sex as more than a mere physical act. It is both an outgrowth of and experience of mutual love. Loving my wife and truly caring for her precedes and actually results in a deep sexual intimacy. In the context of love, we can give ourselves unreservedly to each other."

Even women who were sexually abused as children said that a Christian attitude toward sex enabled them to overcome any negative feelings.

Yet knowledge was not enough for some, as one person explained: "Any good attitudes I had, have come from understanding the biblical teaching on sex, but good attitudes/thoughts don't necessarily overcome negative feelings."

Take your time. Nor surprisingly, couples described time as an ally in their adapting to each other sexually. "The longer we are married, the more I look forward to enjoying sex. My husband becomes more appealing to me sexually as our quantity and quality of shared life experiences accumulate. It is much easier to abandon myself to him. After sex I feel much closer to him emotionally. It has certainly helped me feel good about myself as a woman. I feel secure in his love, and motherhood has been a delight."

Communicate, communicate. Talking about your sensual experience is crucial to improving it.

Wrote one: "We talk together about our feelings during and after our lovemaking. We tell each other which part of the body we need touched and what we feel."

One wife, convinced that her husband would be dissatisfied with her small bust, wrote: "Many of our problems were overcome with time and talking. It was obvious that breast size didn't bother my husband. He enjoyed fondling them and never complained about their size. With practice our performance improved. When I found out that my husband's laugh during climax was of enjoyment and not making fun of me—plus with a little time to adjust to the laugh—it is now a welcome part of our sexual experience."

The wife who was reluctant to tell her husband about having pain during intercourse finally did, gaining his sympathy: "He was caring and very frustrated that I would allow my physical discomfort to go on."

Experiment. One husband wrote that exploration of lovemaking made a difference for him and his wife. "Oral sex was somehow negative at the beginning of our marriage," he wrote. "It's not anymore. The longer we've been married, the more variety we have in our sex life: different positions, oral sex, etc."

Affirm each other. As couples offer unconditional acceptance of each other, they help each other feel better about their sensuality as well as their own bodies. "I was a little bit shameful when I was naked and having sex, but my husband keeps on telling me that I should not be ashamed. His positive and open attitude helped me to reduce my bad feelings."

Talk to a third party. Unable to solve their problems themselves, some couples need to seek help. One wife lacked an appreciation of her body, thinking she didn't measure up to other women. "A crisis time came in our marriage, and I decided I had to change or the marriage would be over. I worked at self-appreciation and was helped mostly by the book by Penner and Penner, *The Gift of Sex.* Both of us went to a Christian counselor and are still working at thoroughly enjoying each other. It took me twenty-nine years and the near catastrophic end of our marriage for me to accept my husband's love as God intended."

Work at it. "My personal experience has shown that a couple can have all the love in the world for each other but not have mastered having sex together. This doesn't mean sex is bad or that there's necessarily a problem in the relationship. It means there is work yet to be done to perfect the area. I think it is when one partner stops working on the sex difficulties that the problem with the relationship begins. Not working in an area so closely tied to one's self-esteem and to so many deep feelings can cause a lack of intimacy and begin to erect barriers."

WHY IT'S WORTH THE EFFORT

Is sex worth the effort? Only you and your partner can answer that. Your marriage is like a masterpiece that the two of you are painting together. It need not look like anyone else's, nor would we insist you follow our suggestions. Sex is not the only way to achieve some of the purposes described in this book. Marriage offers couples many ways to experience love, intimacy, and affirmation. Sex may not be that important to your relationship. What matters most is whether both of you are satisfied. There are, however, some good reasons for continually cultivating your lovemaking.

It's good for your emotional well-being. As therapist Michael Weiner Davis put it, "'Feel good' chemicals are at work when we make love."[1] When in the throes of passion or when having an orgasm, your body releases sex hormones and endorphins that create a sense of elation, stimulating the body's vital organs and glands, promoting a sense of relief and joy.

Sexual activity contributes to our physical health in ways we never understood before. In an article in *Modern Maturity,* the magazine of the American Association of Retired People, Melissa Gotthardt outlined the latest research, proving a romp in the sack is great medicine.[2] One study shows that making love makes the immune system stronger. People who had sex once or twice a week had 30 percent higher levels of immunoglobulin, a substance that battles infections such as colds and stomach viruses.

Sexual pleasure also kills pain. During arousal and orgasm the body produces chemicals that have significant pain-blocking properties. Women who achieved orgasm increased their pain tolerance 75 percent, according to one study.

Regular sex might even extend your life. In a ten-year British study, men who had frequent orgasms had a 50 percent lower death rate than those who didn't.

Would you believe that being sexually active might help you look younger? When a panel of judges was asked to guess the ages of more than three thousand people, those who were most sexually active were the ones the judges said looked seven to ten years younger than their actual age.

While sex alone cannot sustain a marriage or make a bad marriage good, purpose-directed sex can enrich and strengthen a good one. And having a quality marriage will help keep it stable and long lasting.

When asked at what age the sex drive quits, ninety-nine-year-old author Eubie Blake replied, "You'll have to ask somebody older than me."[3] Who knows how long you and your partner will be making love? Surveys of elderly people reveal that their bedroom antics are still quite vigorous. With today's life-expectancy rates, many couples are sexually active for sixty years.

What is happening in your bedroom now will determine what will happen there many years later. Frequent sex floods your sexual machinery with much-needed oxygen-rich blood. "If you are sexually active now," says Irwin Goldstein, M.D., director of the Institute for Sexual Medicine at Boston University of Medicine, "you're protecting your ability to stay that way later."[4]

Isn't the prospect of a lifetime of lovemaking enough of a reason for you to keep it fresh and satisfying? We hope you have already discovered the bliss of making love meaningfully, and if not, that you soon will.

SUGGESTED BOOKS

MARITAL SEX

Danny Akin. *God on Sex: The Creator's Ideas about Love, Intimacy, and Marriage*. Nashville: Broadman & Holman Publishers, 2003. This book sets the many and varied misconceptions about sex alongside God's design to reveal his intention and blessing for this vital dimension of life.

Lonnie Garfield Barbach. *For Yourself: The Fulfillment of Female Sexuality*. New York: Anchor Press, 1976. A practical guide for women who may have trouble expressing their sexuality in marriage.

Tom and Jeannie Elliff. *Letters to Lovers: Wisdom for Every Season of Your Marriage*. Nashville: Broadman & Holman Publishers, 2003. A book that can be used throughout courtship, marriage preparation, and throughout married life for anyone who faces various stages and issues confronting every marriage.

Clifford and Joyce Penner. *Men and Sex*. Nashville: Thomas Nelson, 1997. Should make any man a better husband and lover.

Linda Dillow and Lorraine Pintus. *Intimate Issues: Conversations Woman to Woman: 21 Questions Christian Women Ask About Sex*. Colorado Springs: WaterBrook Press, 1999. A life-changing book for women.

Doug Rosenau. *A Celebration of Sex*. Nashville: Thomas Nelson, 1994. (Revised and Updated edition, November 2002). Written by a trained theologian who has a Ph.D. degree in sex therapy, this book rivals all other Christian books on marital sex.

C. Michael Smith. *Getting Ready for a Lifetime of Love*. Nashville: Broadman & Holman Publishers, 1999. A premarriage workbook for couples that addresses the tough issues and prepares them for marriage.

BOOKS TO HELP RESOLVE ISSUES FROM THE PAST

Dan B. Allender. *The Wounded Heart: Hope for Adult Victims of Childhood Sexual Abuse.* Colorado Springs: Navpress, 1991. The best book on the subject from a Christian point of view.

Dave Carder, ed. *Secrets of Your Family Tree.* Chicago: Moody Press, 1991. Full of insights and practical help.

James Conway. *Adult Children of Divorce.* Downers Grove, Ill.: Inter-Varsity Press, 1990. Comprehensive book by a Christian who really understands the problems of this group of adults.

Janet Woititz. *Struggle for Intimacy.* Pompano Beach, Fla.: Health Communications, Inc., 1985. Analysis of the problem with intimacy that adult children of alcoholics often have, with practical means of improving this area.

NOTES

Chapter 1: Making Sense of the Sensual

1. Jack Morin, *The Erotic Mind: Unlocking the Inner Sources of Sexual Passion and Fulfillment* (New York: HarperPerennial, 1995), 225.

2. Rick Kegan, "Not at a Singles Bar with Erica Jong," *Chicago Tribune,* 18 August 1994, section 5, 1, 3.

3. Kathleen Parker, "Generation Says 'I Don't' to Marriage," *Chicago Tribune,* 12 July 2000, section 1, 33.

4. Ibid.

5. David Knox, *Choices in Relationship* (St. Paul: West, 1985), 81.

6. Esther Crain, "101 Sizzling Secrets of Women Who Love Sex," *Cosmopolitan,* March 2000, 214.

7. Rollo May, *Love and Will* (New York: W. W. Norton & Co., 1969), 37.

8. John T. Noonan, *Contraception: A History of Its Treatment by Catholic Theologians and Canonists* (Cambridge: Harvard University Press, 1966), 126.

9. Ibid.

10. William Kirk Kilpatrick, *The Emperor's New Clothes: The Naked Truth about the New Psychology* (Westchester, Ill.: Crossway, 1985), 64.

11. Morin, *The Erotic Mind,* 125.

12. Mary Ann Lamanna and Agnes Riedmann, *Marriages and Families: Making Choices and Facing Change,* 3rd ed. (Belmont, Calif.: Wadsworth, 1988), 125.

13. George F. Santa, *A Modern Study in the Book of Proverbs: Charles Bridges' Classic Revised for Today's Readers* (Ann Arbor, Mich.: Mott Media, 1978), 70.

Chapter 2: Sex and Intimacy: Looking at Marriage Close-Up

Sections of this chapter were taken from my book *Achieving the Impossible: Intimate Marriage* (Portland, Oreg.: Multnomah Press, 1982).

1. James J. Lynch, *The Broken Heart: The Medical Consequences of Loneliness* (New York: Basic Books, 1977), quoted in Lawrence Crabb, "The Family: Manipulation or Ministry," in *Family Life Education* (Glen Ellyn, Ill.: Scripture Press Ministries, 1978), 9.

2. John Calvin, *Commentary on the First Book of the Bible, Called Genesis* (Grand Rapids, Mich.: Eerdmans, 1963), 128.

3. Mary Pride, *The Way Home: Beyond Feminism, Back to Reality* (Westchester, Ill.: Crossway, 1985), 16, 18.

4. Markus Barth, *Ephesians: Translation and Commentary on Chapters 4–6* (Garden City, N.Y.: Doubleday, 1974), 640.

5. A different word for "friend" is used in the Song of Songs than in Proverbs 2:17.

6. Pierre Mornell, *Passive Men, Wild Women* (New York: Ballantine, 1979), 1–3.

Chapter 3: Sex and Procreation: You Wouldn't Be Without It

1. Andre Guindon, *The Sexual Creators: An Ethical Proposal for Concerned Christians* (New York: University Press of America, 1986), 217.

2. Anthony Kosnik, et al., *Human Sexuality: New Directions in American Catholic Thought* (New York: Paulist, 1977), 34.

3. Ibid., 247.

4. William Granzig and Ellen Peck, *The Parent Test* (New York: Putnam, 1978), 19, quoted in H. Norman Wright and Marvin N. Inmon, *Preparing for Parenthood* (Ventura, Calif.: Regal, 1980), 18–19.

5. "On Having a Family," *The Stony Brook School Bulletin,* February 1981, 1.

6. Deborah R. Baurac, "Aphrodisiacs: Magic or myth?" *Chicago Tribune,* 15 December 1999, section 8, 3.

7. Clifford L. Penner and Joyce J. Penner, *Men and Sex: Discovering Greater Love, Passion and Intimacy with Your Wife* (Nashville: Thomas Nelson, 1997), 75.

8. John Leland with Claudia Kalb and Nadine Joseph, "The Science of Women's Sexuality," *Newsweek,* 29 May 2000, 48–54.

9. Gregg Johnson, "The Biological Basis for Gender-Specific Behavior," in *Recovering Biblical Manhood and Womanhood: A Response to Evangelical Feminism,* eds. John Piper and Wayne Grudem (Wheaton, Ill.: Crossway Books, 1991), 283–84.

10. Ibid., 285.

11. J. Sprague and D. Quadagno, "Gender and Sexual Motivation," *Journal of Psychology and Human Sexuality* (1989, no. 2): 57–76.

12. Johnson, "The Biological Basis for Gender-Specific Behavior," 285.

Chapter 4: Sex and Love: Love Is More Than a Four-Letter Word

1. Elaine Hatfield and G. William Walster, *A New Look at Love* (Reading, Mass.: Addison Wesley), 4.

2. Nathaniel Branden, *The Psychology of Romantic Love* (New York: Bantam, 1980), 3.

3. Ibid.

4. Norman Pittenger, *Love and Control in Sexuality* (Philadelphia: Pilgram, 1974), 122.

5. H. S. Sullivan, *Conceptions of Modern Psychiatry,* 2nd ed. (New York: Norton, 1966), 42–43.

6. Gibson Winter, *Love and Conflict* (New York: Doubleday, 1958) quoted in Helen Koiman Hosie, *The Other Side of Divorce* (New York: Hawthorn, 1974), 141.

7. Sonnet 103, *The Love Poems and Sonnets of William Shakespeare* (Garden City, N.J.: Doubleday, 1957), 60.

8. Mary Pride, *The Way Home: Beyond Feminism, Back to Reality* (Westchester, Ill.: Crossway, 1985), 20.

9. Anne E. Kazak and N. Dickon Reppucci, "Romantic Love as a Social Institution," in *On Love and Loving: Psychological Perspectives on the Nature and Experience of Romantic Love,* ed. Kenneth S. Pope (San Francisco: Jossey-Bass, 1980), 213.

10. Gary Chapman describes these in his book *The Five Love Languages: How to Express Your Heartfelt Commitment to Your Mate* (Chicago: Northfield, 1996).

Chapter 5: Sex and Personal Identity: Affirmation Matters

1. Mary Ann Lamanna and Agnes Riedmann, *Marriages and Families: Making Choices and Facing Change,* 3rd ed. (Belmont, Calif.: Wadsworth, 1988), 121.

2. Ibid.

3. Clifford L. Penner and Joyce J. Penner, *Men and Sex: Discovering Greater Love, Passion, and Intimacy with Your Wife* (Nashville: Thomas Nelson, 1997), 76–77.

4. Jack Morin, *The Erotic Mind: Unlocking the Inner Sources of Sexual Passion and Fulfillment* (New York: HarperPerennial, 1995), 143–44.

5. J. M. Gottman, *What Predicts Divorce? The Relationship Between Marital Processes and Marital Outcomes* (Hillsdale, N.J.: Lawrence Erlbaum, 1994).

6. Michael Gross, "The Lethal Politics of Beauty: Why Women Are Dying to Look This Good," *George,* June 2000, 56.

7. Ibid., 58.

8. Ibid., 54.

9. Ibid.

Chapter 6: Sex and Pleasure: Drink Deep of Love

1. Joan Elizabeth Loyd, "Quickies Are the Big Macs of the Sex World," *Cosmopolitan,* May 2000, 168.

2. Mary Pride, *The Way Home: Beyond Feminism, Back to Reality* (Wheaton, Ill.: Crossway, 1985), 18.

3. David Mace and Vera Mace, *The Sacred Fire: Christian Marriage Through the Ages* (Nashville: Abingdon, 1986), 135.

4. Derrick Sherwin Bailey, *Sexual Relation in Christian Thought* (New York: Harper & Brothers, 1959), 169–70.

5. Norman Pittenger, *Love and Control in Sexuality* (Philadelphia: Pilgrim, 1974), 28.

6. Franz Von Streng, *Marriage* (New York: Benzinger Brothers, 1939), 103.

7. Peter Gardella, *Innocent Ecstasy: How Christianity Gave America an Ethic of Sexual Pleasure* (New York: Oxford University Press, 1985), 55.

8. Ibid., 56.

9. Gardella, *Innocent Ecstasy,* 58.

10. Ibid., 47.

11. Ibid., 61.

12. Daniel S. Stein, *Passionate Sex: Discover the Special Power in You* (New York: Carroll and Graf, 2000), from the book cover.

13. Ibid., 8.

14. Marian E. Dunn, quoted in Jennifer Cadoff, "Have the Best Sex of Your Life," *McCall's,* June 2000, 73 and following.

15. Pride, *The Way Home,* 24.

16. Judy Dillow, *Solomon on Sex* (New York: Thomas Nelson, 1977), 31.

17. Jack Morin, *The Erotic Mind: Unlocking the Inner Sources of Sexual Passion and Fulfillment* (New York: HarperPerennial, 1995), 15.

18. Ibid., 57.

19. Dunn, quoted in Cadoff, "Have the Best Sex of Your Life," 73.

Chapter 7: Sex and Prevention: Delivering Us from Evil

1. John White, *Eros Defiled* (Downers Grove, Ill.: InterVarsity Press, 1977), 10.

2. David and Vera Mace, *The Sacred Fire: Christian Marriage Throughout the Ages* (Nashville: Abingdon, 1986), 129.

3. Barbara Tuchman, *A Distant Mirror: The Calamitous Fourteenth Century* (New York: Ballantine, 1978), 31.

4. Esmein Adhemar, *Le Marriage en Droit Canonique,* ed. R. Genestal (Paris, 1929–1935), quoted in Frances Gies and Joseph Gies, *Marriage and the Family in the Middle Ages* (New York: Harper & Row, 1987), 155.

5. *Sexual Health Update* 7, no 3 (fall 1999): 12.

6. Ibid.

7. A. C. Kinsey, W. B. Pomeroy, and C. E. Martin, *Sexual Behavior in the Human Male* (Philadelphia: W. B. Saunders, 1948).

8. Robert T. Michael, *Sex in America: A Definitive Survey* (Boston: Little, Brown, 1994), 88–89, in *Sexual Health Update,* 12.

9. Andrew M. Greeley, *Faithful Attraction: Discovering Intimacy, Love, and Fidelity in American Marriage* (New York: Tom Douherty Associates, 1991).

10. Nobile, Phillip, and Edward Eichel, *The Perfect Fit* (New York: Penguin Books, 1993), 99.

11. Patrick Carnes, *Don't Call It Love: Recovery from Sexual Addiction* (New York: Bantam, 1991), 42.

12. Harry W. Schaumburg, *False Intimacy: Understanding the Struggle of Sexual Addiction* (Colorado Springs, Colo.: Navpress, 1992), 62–65.

Conclusion: Sexual Adjustment: In Their Words

1. Michele Weiner Davis, *The Sex-Starved Marriage: A Couple's Guide to Boosting Their Marriage Libido* (N.Y.: Simon and Schuster, 2003), 33.

2. Melissa Gotthardt, "Sexual Healing," *Modern Maturity,* January/February 2003, 14.

3. Eubie Blake, 1883–1983. Ned Sherrin in *The Oxford Dictionary of Humorous Quotations* (Oxford: Oxford University Press, 2d ed., 2001), 178.

4. Gotthardt, "Sexual Healing," 15.